FROM THE
GREAT [
TO AM

The Last Memoir

MIKE CARNEY (Micheál Ó Ceárna), born in 1920 on The Great Blasket Island, emigrated to the Hungry Hill neighbourhood of Springfield, Massachusetts in 1948. He knew little English when he travelled to the mainland at sixteen. In Dublin he worked as a barman and wrote an Irish-language column for *The Irish Press*. In Springfield, he worked as a grocery store manager and as a security officer. He was president of the John Boyle O'Reilly Club for sixteen years and helped to create the Blasket Island Centre (Dunquin). He was awarded an honorary doctoral degree in Celtic literature from the National University of Ireland Maynooth in 2009, honouring his lifelong devotion to preserving the language and culture of his native place.

GERALD HAYES is married to Mike's daughter Maureen. He visits West Kerry frequently with his family and makes the trip over to The Great Blasket itself whenever weather conditions allow. Hayes is a retired vice-president of Westfield State University in Massachusetts.

These memoirs are dedicated:

- To Seán Tom Ó Ceárna and Neilí Uí Cheárna, my father and mother, for inspiring me to pursue my dreams.
- To my beloved sister Cáit who raised us with a mother's care and affection and who sacrificed much so that we would grow up healthy and wise.
- To my dear brother Seán, who died on The Great Blasket Island at the age of twenty-four. His death led to the evacuation of the island. And to my brother Seámus who died before we even knew him.
- To my other brothers and sisters, both living and deceased, Maurice, Martin, Paddy, Maureen, Tom and Billy, with whom I shared the adventure of emigration and who collectively established a new home for the Ó Ceárna/Carney/Kearney family in the United States.
- To my courageous forebears, particularly my great aunt Nellie Carney, the first of my family to emigrate to America. They paved the way for me and my family to relocate from Ireland and to build a better life for ourselves and our descendants.
- To the Ó Cinnéide family of Moorestown, County Kerry, and to all who collaborated in the preservation of The Great Blasket Island, its history, its literature and its spirit. They created institutions that will keep the memory of the island alive forever.
- To my children and their families who are a source of enormous pride and who themselves have worked hard to advance the preservation and memory of the island.
- And finally, to the love of my life, my deceased wife Maureen Ward Carney. This Roscommon woman put up with my passion for The Great Blasket Island for more than sixty years. She had the grace of Mary and patience of Job. I miss her so.

MICHAEL J. CARNEY
(MICHEÁL J. Ó CEÁRNA)

Index

From The
Great Blasket
to America

The Last Memoir by an Islander

MICHAEL CARNEY with GERALD HAYES

2015

*Hope you enjoy this tale
of a remarkable islander . . .
Sláinte !
Michael O'Ceanna* Jy Hayes

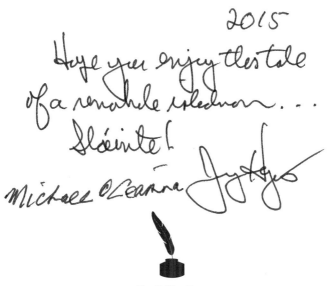

The Collins Press

FIRST PUBLISHED IN 2013 BY
The Collins Press
West Link Park
Doughcloyne
Wilton
Cork

Reprinted 2013

British Library Cataloguing in Publication Data
Carney, Michael J., 1920–
From The Great Blasket to America: the last memoir by an islander.
1. Carney, Michael J., 1920– 2. Great Blasket Island (Ireland)—
Biography. 3. Irish—Massachusetts—Springfield—Biography.
I. Title II. Hayes, Gerald.
941.9'6-dc23

ISBN–13: 9781848891654

Maps by Dómhnal Ó Bric, Dún Chaoin

Typesetting by Carrigboy Typesetting Services

Typeset in Garamond Premier Pro 11.5pt/14pt

Printed in Malta by Gutenberg Press Limited

Contents

Cover photographs

Front (main and spine): The Great Blasket Island (Kevin Farnan); *top (l–r):* Mike Carney's father, stands in front of his house on The Great Blasket (Thomas H. Mason); Blasket Island boys pose for a photo. Mike Carney is standing, far left, with his brothers Tom, Martin and Paddy sitting in front (Blasket Centre Archives); A&P store on Main Street, Springfield, Massachusetts (Springfield Public Library). *Back (l–r):* a view of The Great Blasket Island, looking northeastwards (Blasket Centre Archives); Mike Carney (right) with his sponsor, his uncle Tom Carney, in 1948 (Carney family archive); island children on the strand. Mike Carney is second from left (Blasket Centre Archives).

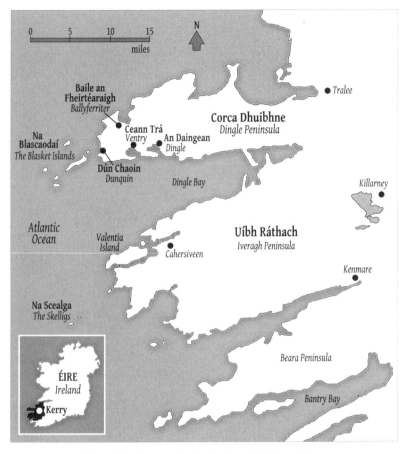

Map of West Kerry showing the location of the Blasket Islands.

Introduction

Mike Carney is my father-in-law. More importantly, Mike Carney is my friend. When I met Mike almost thirty years ago, I had never heard of The Great Blasket Island. Mike was incredulous that anyone who claimed Irish heritage (I am half-Irish) could possibly be ignorant of such a significant aspect of Irish history. He was more than a little wary of me.

I achieved a breakthrough with Mike when we realised that he had been friendly with my by-then-deceased grandfather, Daniel J. Hayes, who had lived to be a spry ninety-seven. Dan was quite fond of a pint of Guinness and a shot of whiskey at the John Boyle O'Reilly Club in Springfield, Massachusetts, on an occasional Sunday afternoon. An emigrant himself, Dan was a bit of a local celebrity in his own right. He and Mike would relax and share the boundless joys of Irish heritage on those Sunday afternoons many years ago. Mike let me know in no uncertain terms, however, that my grandfather was from Limerick (the village of Effin, Kilmallock) and that Limerick was, by definition, far inferior to the glorious Kingdom of Kerry.

As we became closer, Mike took to calling me, affectionately I'm sure, a 'goddamned narrowback'. At the time, I thought he was drawing a contrast between the physical attributes of those like me who grew up in the relatively soft environs of the United States with those like him, who had endured the rigours of life on a sparse island off the coast of Ireland and had the broad back to prove it. But now it seems that he was simply comparing my American birth with the genuine article, an Irish immigrant, a so-called 'greenhorn'.

The fact that I married his daughter Maureen was not sufficient to seal the deal. I had to be educated about The Great Blasket. Out

came the photos and the stories . . . and more stories. I was surprised by my level of interest in what turned out to be a fascinating saga. Tell me more about 'The Great *Blasted* island,' I would tease him. Little did I know that the word 'Blasted' actually reflected his own personal view of the derivation of the word 'Blasket'.

Over the years, Mike introduced me to two ardent Blasket stalwarts living in Ireland: Edna Uí Chinnéide of Moorestown in County Kerry and her son, Micheál Ó Cinnéide, currently of County Wexford. Edna is the widow of Caoimhín Ó Cinnéide, Mike's second cousin and one of his best friends in Dublin where they both lived during their twenties. Edna and Micheál are dedicated and tireless patrons of all things Blasket. They have been extraordinarily kind, generous and patient as I expanded my Blasket knowledge.

Then there were trips to Ireland and to The Great Blasket Island itself. My wife Maureen and I were profoundly moved by finally standing in the ruins of the long-abandoned Carney home on the island, together with our children, Michael and Andrew. We also gained a fuller appreciation of the significance of the Blaskets during an elongated personal tour of the Blasket Centre (*Ionad an Bhlascaoid*), courtesy of its director, Micheál de Mórdha.

Later, my wife and I pitched in with her cousin and Blasket descendant, Sean Cahillane of Springfield, to coalesce support for the creation of The Great Blasket Island National Historical Park among descendants of the participants in the Blasket diaspora. This effort is gradually coming to fruition after more than ten years of sustained effort on both sides of the Atlantic.

At some point in our relationship, Mike inexplicably switched the way he referred to me. Instead of addressing me as a 'narrowback', he began to call me either 'Captain' or 'Doctor', depending on his whim. I took that as a subtle affirmation that my Blasket immersion was complete. While I will never be an 'islander', I have gained from Mike Carney an appreciation for the true meaning of the term.

These memoirs stem from a realisation that the story of the Blaskets and the interrelated story of Mike's own life as an Irish

emigrant are really quite remarkable. After hearing anecdotes of island life and of his personal journey to America for many years, I eventually recognised that Mike's story is worthy of preservation. In the winter of 2008/2009, I decided that I had procrastinated long enough. Mike and I undertook a series of Saturday morning interviews eventually totalling more than twenty-five hours. His often vivid recall at the age of eighty-eight was extraordinary, especially considering the fact that he left the island at the age of sixteen. I then sorted the interviews and filled the gaps to create a coherent storyline. While the story is Mike's, I edited the overall flow for readability.

To some extent, this collaborative writing process is reminiscent of the literary interaction that earlier island authors undertook with their collaborators: Tomás Ó Criomhthain with Robin Flower; Muiris Ó Súilleabháin with George Thomson; and Peig Sayers with her son Micheál Ó Guithín.

Since we approached the exercise as a memoir, this story presents Mike's lifelong memories and personal perspectives in the first person. It is not, in any way, a disciplined history in the traditional sense. It is pure Mike Carney. It is entirely possible that Mike's memory of details may have failed him and he might be guilty of embellishment from time to time, but the underlying story is an accurate portrayal of a fascinating life.

One interesting aspect of island life is a series of apparent contradictions and clear contrasts. They include: the physical beauty of The Great Blasket with the harsh living conditions endured by its people; the happy singing of Mike's mother with her yearning for her family off-island in Coumeenole; and the uncomplaining approach to life with folk music characterised by lamenting. A more practical contradiction involved living on an island and making a living by fishing on dangerous seas with the fact that few learned how to swim.

These contradictions suggest a quiet discontent that must have been a factor in the acceleration of emigration from the island. Mike acknowledges these issues, but he shrugs and accepts them as a reflection of the reality of island life.

Perhaps the most vivid example of the prevailing ambivalence toward the island is Mike's father's emigrating to America, not once but twice, and moving back to the island both times.

One constant in Mike's life has been his unrelenting pressuring of the Irish government. From 1947 to 1953 he was involved in trying to persuade the government to evacuate The Great Blasket Island. Then, over the last twenty years or so, he has been involved in persuading the government to preserve the island properly and recognise its contribution to Irish culture. Mike disavows any interest in politics, yet he has certainly developed the persistence and tenacity of a lobbyist in the pursuit of his goals.

One editorial struggle involved the use of the word 'emigrant' rather than 'immigrant' and associated derivations of each. It was a close call, but ultimately I chose to use 'emigrant' because this is Mike's story and he views himself more as an emigrant from Ireland than an immigrant to the United States. Case closed.

To respect the authenticity of Mike's voice, some of his routine conversational expressions are incorporated in the narrative. For example, when referring to past events, Mike will often say 'in them days'. When referring to people going over to the island, he invariably uses the preposition 'into'. I hope that these nuances and others add to the flavour of the story.

Finally, there is the matter of language. I have found Irish, frequently referred to as 'Gaelic', to be a challenge. It operates on its own alphabet of eighteen letters and there are multiple local dialects. There are even variations in the exact spelling of certain words and names. Nevertheless, in order to add to the authenticity of this work, I have tried valiantly to include the Irish spellings for names, places, artifacts and selected expressions that seem closest to the local Irish convention in West Kerry. The Irish is presented in parentheses immediately after the first use of a particular name, word or expression. For names, I have included the most commonly used version, either Irish or English, and provided both versions where individuals changed their common name over time. My apologies if I have mangled a name or a word or two . . . or more.

I hope you will agree that Mike Carney's story is particularly poignant because of his stature as the oldest and one of the last surviving native Blasket Islanders. At the time of writing, there are only ten islanders remaining, seven in Ireland and three in America, including Mike and his sister Maureen Carney Oski.

Let me acknowledge the terrific work of Cole Moreton in his book *Hungry for Home, Leaving the Blaskets: A Journey from the Edge of Ireland*. Moreton chronicles the 1953 evacuation of The Great Blasket Island and related events. His work is based, in part, on his own interviews with Mike, his sister Cáit and his brothers Paddy and Martin – as well as other Springfield-area Blasket descendants, including Sean Cahillane. Regrettably, Cáit, Paddy and Martin are now deceased.

The publication of this book in 2013 coincides with the sixtieth anniversary of the evacuation and the twentieth anniversary of the opening of the Blasket Centre. It is altogether fitting to publish a new Blasket memoir at this time to help mark these significant milestones.

This memoir differs from other books in the Blasket library in at least two respects. Firstly, it encompasses the emigration of an islander to America and his subsequent efforts to preserve the legacy of the Blaskets. And, secondly, it is also likely to be the last book written by a Blasket writer. I hope that this work is a fitting contribution to this long and captivating tradition.

I will concede at the outset that this written account cannot possibly capture the charm of the story as told by Mike himself. There is something about the lilt in his voice, the twinkle in his eye and his hearty chuckle that communicate his pride, passion and emotion. Such are the limitations of the written word.

I hope that I have done justice to the man and to his story. After all, Mike Carney is my friend.

GERALD W. HAYES

The Ó Ceárna

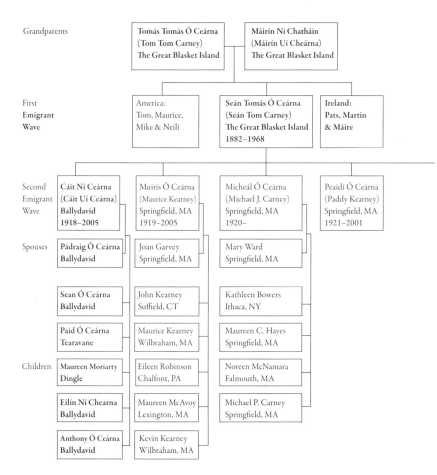

Grandparents	**Tomás Tomás Ó Ceárna** (Tom Tom Carney) The Great Blasket Island	**Máirín Ní Chatháin** (Máirín Uí Cheárna) The Great Blasket Island	

First Emigrant Wave

- America: Tom, Maurice, Mike & Neilí
- **Seán Tomás Ó Ceárna** (Seán Tom Carney) The Great Blasket Island 1882–1968
- Ireland: Pats, Martin & Máire

Second Emigrant Wave

| **Cáit Ní Ceárna** (Cáit Uí Cheárna) **Ballydavid** **1918–2005** | Muiris Ó Ceárna (Maurice Kearney) Springfield, MA 1919–2005 | Micheál Ó Ceárna (Michael J. Carney) Springfield, MA 1920– | Peaidí Ó Ceárna (Paddy Kearney) Springfield, MA 1921–2001 |

Spouses

| **Pádraig Ó Ceárna** **Ballydavid** | Joan Garvey Springfield, MA | Mary Ward Springfield, MA | |

Children

Sean Ó Ceárna **Ballydavid**	John Kearney Suffield, CT	Kathleen Bowers Ithaca, NY
Paíd Ó Ceárna **Tearavane**	Maurice Kearney Wilbraham, MA	Maureen C. Hayes Springfield, MA
Maureen Moriarty **Dingle**	Eileen Robinson Chalfont, PA	Noreen McNamara Falmouth, MA
Eilín Ní Chearna **Ballydavid**	Maureen McAvoy Lexington, MA	Michael P. Carney Springfield, MA
Anthony Ó Ceárna **Ballydavid**	Kevin Kearney Wilbraham, MA	

Principal residence in West Kerry = **Bold**
October 2012

The Ó Ceárna Family Tree

FAMILY TREE

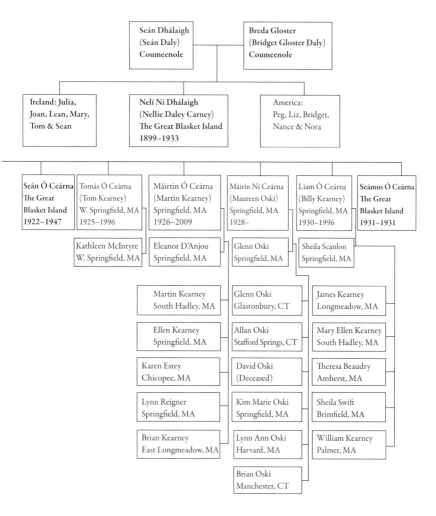

Seán Dhálaigh
(Seán Daly)
Coumeenole

Breda Gloster
(Bridget Gloster Daly)
Coumeenole

Ireland: Julia,
Joan, Lean, Mary,
Tom & Sean

Nelí Ní Dhálaigh
(Nellie Daley Carney)
The Great Blasket Island
1899–1933

America:
Peg, Liz, Bridget,
Nance & Nora

Seán Ó Ceárna
The Great
Blasket Island
1922–1947

Tomás Ó Ceárna
(Tom Kearney)
W. Springfield, MA
1925–1996

Máirtin Ó Ceárna
(Martin Kearney)
Springfield, MA
1926–2009

Máirín Ní Ceárna
(Maureen Oski)
Springfield, MA
1928–

Liam Ó Ceárna
(Billy Kearney)
Springfield, MA
1930–1996

Seámus Ó Ceárna
The Great
Blasket Island
1931–1931

Kathleen McIntyre
W. Springfield, MA

Eleanor D'Anjou
Springfield, MA

Glenn Oski
Springfield, MA

Sheila Scanlon
Springfield, MA

Martin Kearney
South Hadley, MA

Glenn Oski
Glastonbury, CT

James Kearney
Longmeadow, MA

Ellen Kearney
Springfield, MA

Allan Oski
Stafford Springs, CT

Mary Ellen Kearney
South Hadley, MA

Karen Estey
Chicopee, MA

David Oski
(Deceased)

Theresa Beaudry
Amherst, MA

Lynn Reigner
Springfield, MA

Kim Marie Oski
Springfield, MA

Sheila Swift
Brimfield, MA

Brian Kearney
East Longmeadow, MA

Lynn Ann Oski
Harvard, MA

William Kearney
Palmer, MA

Brian Oski
Manchester, CT

1. The Most Beautiful Place on Earth

The Great Blasket Island (*An Blascaod Mór*) is located about 3 miles off the southwest coast of County Kerry. It is one of the westernmost points of land in all of Europe. The island is about 3½ miles long and half a mile wide, about 1,100 acres in all. At its highest point, it is about a thousand feet above sea level.

The Great Blasket's beauty is breathtaking. The whole area, including the island itself and the Dingle Peninsula (*Corca Dhuibhne*), has been called 'the most beautiful place on earth' by *National Geographic Traveler*. I couldn't agree more.

This island is my homeland. Even at almost ninety-three years of age, I dream about it almost every night.

The first thing I see in my dreams is the white sandy beach (*an tráigh bháin*) on the coast of the island facing the mainland. When we were children, we used to roll up our trousers and run in the surf or play Gaelic football and other sports on the beach that we called 'the strand'. This is the only fairly flat land on the whole island. To the right and left of the beach is a coastline of black jagged rock running north and south with cliffs averaging about 30 feet high.

Blasket Sound is called '*An Bealach*'. The water is very rough with lots of rocks and reefs, many of them hidden under the surface of the water. It is a treacherous place and navigation is very tricky, even for the most experienced sailors. Over the years, there were a large number of shipwrecks in the Sound. A ship from the Spanish Armada, the *Santa Maria de la Rosa*, sank here in 1588 and there is a stone monument over on the mainland commemorating its wreck. Other shipwrecks included the *Lochie*, the *Commerce*, the *Caroline* and the *Quebra*. These are dangerous waters indeed.

The Great Blasket Island, centre left, with Inishvickillane to the far left, Beginish and Tearaght to the right. The village of Dunquin is in the foreground.

At the left of the beach in a small cove is the only island pier (*Caladh an Oileáin*) with a slipway. It is hidden from view as you approach the island, behind a large rock. It is very risky trying to get a boat of any type into or away from the pier. Even today, you have to bless yourself before you make your landing!

There is a well-worn clay path leading from the pier up a short distance to the village. The homes were built on the rising slope looking out in an easterly direction across the Sound towards the small mainland community of Dunquin *(Dún Chaoin)*. The island village is clustered in a small area. There are two sections: '*bun an bhaile*', the bottom of the village, and '*barr an bhaile*', the top of the village. The bottom section is close enough to the Sound that you can hear the waves constantly crashing on the shore, especially in bad weather.

The island was occupied for hundreds of years until it was evacuated by the Irish government in 1953. The first known inhabitants were probably monks or maybe even Vikings. They left behind a few stone beehive huts and an old stone fort on one of the island's two peaks. Later, after the English takeover of Ireland in the sixteenth century, the island was owned by the Earl of Cork.

There was an influx of people from the mainland into the island when land rents were going up all over Ireland in the early 1800s. Tenant farmers couldn't afford to pay their rent and bailiffs

Aerial view of the island village in 2012 showing the ruins of the homes, the Congested District Board houses at the top of the village, the roadways and the fields.

representing the landowners came around chasing people for money. It was a big controversy. Some people went into the island from the mainland to avoid the unaffordable rents.

The islanders used to tell stories about a bailiff from the Earl of Cork coming into the island to collect rent. It seems that the bailiff was stoned from the cliff above the pier by the women of the island and he went away without any money. At some point, the bailiff just gave up. There wasn't enough money to be raised for the amount of aggravation involved. So, in effect, the land on the island was mostly free of charge.

The Congested Districts Board, an agency of the British government charged with improving living conditions, bought the island from the Earl of Cork in 1907 – for just a few hundred pounds. At that point, the land was divided among the islanders with twenty-five families each receiving a house, a small field and rights to use the common land. The islanders became landowners!

Sadly, the young people of the island were never taught about its history as we were growing up. We didn't talk about specific

View of the island village in 2012 from Blasket Sound. Note that the village is situated in a kind of a bowl that helped protect it from the wind – to some extent.

dates and events involving the island in them days. Everything was just hearsay. The islanders used to say that the Great Famine that occurred in Ireland in the mid-1800s hit the island too, but not as bad as in the rest of Ireland. I suppose it was because of the physical separation from the mainland; maybe the blight that infected Ireland's potato crop did not travel across the Sound to the island.

In its heyday in the early 1900s, about 175 people lived on the island. When I left the island in 1937, the population was down to about 110. By 1947, the population was about fifty or so. When the island was evacuated in 1953, there were only twenty-two left. It was a long, gradual and very sad decline.

There were only about thirty houses on the island. Most of the houses were built of whitewashed stone with black felt roofs coated with tar. In my days on the island, it was easy to see the bright, white houses of the village all the way from Dunquin. Today, the weather has worn away the old whitewash from the buildings and the bare grey stones of the old, abandoned and partially collapsed homes are only visible in part from the mainland.

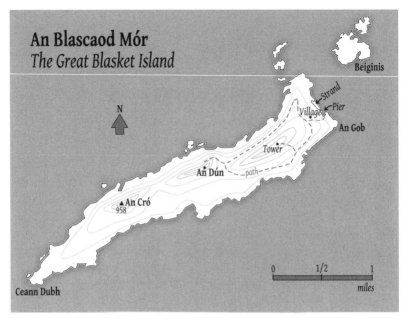

Map of The Great Blasket Island.

A little farther up the hill, just beyond the stone houses, were five large white concrete houses that were built by the Congested Districts Board in 1909 to improve housing on the island. The islanders called them 'the new houses'. Even today, you can still easily see these white buildings from over on the mainland. Up the hill from the village and to the north is the sloped land we used for farming. Each family had its own plot for growing potatoes and other vegetables. The land was laid out in a grid pattern that looked like a chequerboard from the higher elevations. Along the side of the hill is a large area of common land where sheep were grazed.

There is a high ridge running along the length of the island from east to west starting behind the village and continuing all the way to the western tip of the island. At the top of this ridge are two peaks, called the Fort (*An Dún*) and the Crow (*An Cró*). The Fort is the ruins of the old abandoned fortification that may have been

5

built by Vikings. There used to be an old tower up on the ridge, but it was struck by lightning and collapsed when I was about twelve years old. The Crow is the highest point on the island. Farther towards the back of the island, the land falls down sharply to the Atlantic Ocean on all sides.

When I was young, I used to hike up to the Crow on a clear day, just for the spectacular view of the scenery across the whole bay. You could see the Irish coastline all the way from the Three Sisters, (*Na Triúr Deirfiúr*) the hills on the mainland to the north, to Slea Head (*Ceann Sléibhe*), the high bluff to the south. In the middle, you could see the top of Mount Eagle (*Sliabh an Iolair*), the highest point on the west end of the Dingle Peninsula and Dunmore Head (*An Dún Mór*).

At the back of the island, to the west, is Black Head (*Ceann Dubh*), overlooking the neighbouring island of Inishvickillane. There was great rabbit hunting and fishing out there on that part of the island. On the coastline, there are huge rock cliffs, about 30 or 40 foot tall, that drop straight down into the ocean.

There are lots of caves along the cliffs. The most famous is 'Feiritéar's Cave' (*Scairt Phiarais*), the secret place where the famous Piaras Feiritéar, the politician, revolutionary and poet, once hid out when the English Army under Oliver Cromwell was chasing after him way back in the 1600s. Eventually, though, the British captured him on the mainland and hanged the poor man over in Killarney in 1653.

One day when I was a boy I visited Feiritéar's Cave with my best friend Maurice Guiheen. It was a daredevil kind of thing to do. If you slipped on the path, you'd fall right down the cliff. It was very dark and damp inside with water dripping from the ceiling. My brother Martin made the same tour and wrote his name on the wall of the cave. Dáithí de Mórdha of the Blasket Centre made the trek to the cave in 2012 and found Martin's name still on the wall along with that of my father, Seán Tom Ó Ceárna.

The island is one of a group of six called the Blasket Islands (*Na Blascaodaí*):

- The Great Blasket Island, my homeland, the largest of the group by far.
- Beginish (*Beiginis*), the small, low island located about a quarter of a mile east of The Great Blasket towards the mainland. It had a single house at one time and was used primarily for grazing sheep. But it has no fresh water.
- Inishnabro (*Inis na Bró*), a mountainous island located to the west of The Great Blasket. It was full of wild birds and rabbits. Its high rocks look like the spires of a cathedral.
- Inishvickillane (*Inis Mhic Uibhleáin*), the westernmost of the Blaskets, a flat island with a house that was once owned by the politician Charlie Haughey, a former Taoiseach (or Prime Minister to my American friends). This island is still owned by his family. Haughey bought it from the Daly family who formerly lived on The Great Blasket.
- Inishtooskert (*Inis Tuaisceart*), called 'The Sleeping Giant' because its shape in the ocean looks like a big person sleeping on his back. It is the northernmost of the Blaskets and is another great place for wild birds and rabbits. We used it for grazing sheep. I spent a couple of nights out there once while fetching sheep for shearing.
- Tearaght (*An Tiaracht*), a small island sticking straight up out of the water. It has a lighthouse that is now automated. There is a narrow archway on Tearaght that only the most skilled oarsman would paddle through in a *naomhóg,* the ocean-going currach used by the islanders.

Of these six islands, only The Great Blasket Island was occupied for any length of time. The other islands are sometimes called the 'Lesser Blaskets'. They are just too wild and remote for long-term living.

There were no trees on The Great Blasket, but it was covered with other thick vegetation. It is a beautiful deep green in the summer and an off-green, just a little brownish, in the winter. But the island is never as green as the mainland because of the saltwater mist from the ocean. The rock cliffs on the island are as black as the

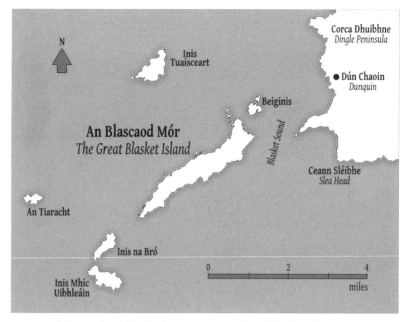

Map showing the Blasket Islands with Dunquin to the right (east) on the mainland.

ace of spades. There were about five small streams on the island, but no ponds. These streams and our two spring-fed wells were the sources of fresh water.

The island is quite a spectacular place, with its broad view of the sky, the Atlantic Ocean, the mainland, the other islands, and its own beach. My late friend Tom Biuso, a professor from Colby Sawyer College in New Hampshire in America, one of the regular visitors to West Kerry and a great friend of the island, used to say that when you look at the island from Dunquin, it looks like a huge whale swimming in the ocean.

Dunquin is the nearest village on the mainland, located at the very tip of the Dingle Peninsula. Dingle (*An Daingean*) is by far the biggest town on the peninsula. It is about 12 miles southeast of Dunquin, past Slea Head and Ventry *(Ceann Trá)*, along the shore of Dingle Bay. The village of Ballyferriter (*Baile an Fheirtéaraigh*)

View of the island, looking northeastwards, with the Congested Districts Board houses to the left and the strand to the right.

is about 5 miles northeast of Dunquin in the opposite direction along the shore road.

While the scenery was beautiful, island life involved quite a lot of hardship. It was a tough existence because of the bad weather, the rough ocean and the isolation. Weather was very important on the island because the people made their living fishing out on the ocean. When high winds and rain kicked up, you couldn't go fishing, or go get the mail in Dunquin, or go to Mass on a Sunday at St Gobnet's Church over on the mainland. Weather was a big problem. In fact, I think that the word 'Blasket' came from the word 'blasted', referring to the weather. The weather was a never-ending threat on the island. Since the weather was usually against the islanders, we were always complaining about it. But the people

The Ó Ceárna home (second building from the left) with its small addition on the right. The island school is just visible on the left.

living on the island didn't think life was so bad. The weather and the remote location were part of our way of living, and we were quite content with the situation for many, many years.

The island economy was based on fishing. Mackerel and herring were caught and sold in Dingle. In the summer, lobster and crawfish were the big catch. The fact that the men of the island were fishermen was written in their skin. Their weathered skin, especially on their faces, showed the result of their constant exposure to the wind and the salt water.

The island was a 'bare-knuckle' place. There was no police department, no courthouse, no post office, no general shop, no doctor, no electricity, no running water, no church and no pub. The islanders had to make do with what they had, which was not much. I maintain that the island people were saintly, but didn't know it. We lived quietly among ourselves. We were hard-working. We got along well together. We were very understanding and accepting of our situation.

But, eventually, some islanders began to realise that there might be a better way of living on the mainland or perhaps in America. They began to be enticed by visions of a better life for them and their families. I remember islanders saying, 'you can't eat the view'. It's sad, but true.

There were, of course, other island communities situated off the west coast of Ireland, like the Aran Islands off Galway, Tory off Donegal and Inishturk off Mayo. But The Great Blasket is quite different because of the enormous body of literature that came from the island.

In my dreams, I remember the island as a happy place. Maybe we didn't know any better. I still get nostalgic over it. After all these many, many years, I still miss it dearly.

To me, the island today looks lonely all by itself in the ocean with nobody living there, especially in comparison to when I was growing up there. It was so lively then. It is my belief that the island doesn't deserve to be lonely like that. I would like to see it go back to the way it was, a lively community of friendly people. Well, I suppose I can always dream.

2. Mike Carney: Islandman

My baptismal name is Micheál Ó Ceárna (Mike Carney). I was born on 22 September 1920, in our house on the The Great Blasket Island. I was the third of ten children. My father was Seán Tom Ó Ceárna (Sean Tom Carney), a native islander. My mother was Neilí Ní Dhálaigh who was born and raised in Coumeenole (*Com Dhineoil)* over on the mainland, just south of Dunquin near Slea Head.

The practice on the island was for babies to be born at home with the help of a midwife. There was no doctor on the island unless there was a serious problem of some nature, and even then only if the weather was such that the doctor could get over to the island. I was delivered by Méiní Uí Dhuinnshléibhe who assisted at most of the island births in them days.

I was baptised when I was four days old in St Vincent's Church in Ballyferriter. I imagine my parents took me to the mainland by *naomhóg* and then to the church in Ballyferriter by horse and cart. My godfather was Seámus Ó Duinnshléibhe, a family friend, and my godmother was Eilín Ní Cheárna, my aunt. I have an official baptismal certificate. But I have never been able to get a birth certificate from the government. The Kerry County Council can't seem to find a record of my birth. I suppose it is possible that a record was never filed with the government years ago. The islanders did not worry too much about government records. They had far bigger issues to deal with.

As far as I know, four generations of my family lived on the island. My great-grandfather Pádraig Ó Ceárna may have been the

A certificate documenting Mike Carney's baptism at St Vincent's Church.

first member of my family to live on the island. This was in the early 1800s. I don't know whether he was born on the island or moved into the island. There is some uncertainty about this because islanders never wrote down things like that. But I do know that my grandfather and my father were born on the island.

My grandfather was Tomás 'Pats' Ó Ceárna because his first name was Tom and his father's first name was Pats. He was born in 1851. My father was called Seán Tom Ó Ceárna. Seán was his first name and Tom was his father's first name. He was born in 1882. The islanders picked up this naming habit so that you did not confuse people. To remember names, the islanders used your first name, and your father's first name, and sometimes your grandfather's first name. This was because quite a few families had the same surname and a lot of people had the same first names too. For example, there were two different Ó Cearna clans with three Ó Cearna families in each clan. People used your family lineage in your name to be clear.

Mike Carney at about twenty-four years of age wearing a 'Fáinne Oir', a gold circular lapel pin from the Gaelic League signifying that he spoke Irish.

On the island, I was called 'Mike Seán Tom Ó Ceárna'. We did not have given middle names on the island. I took the middle name of 'Joseph' after I came to America.

My grandfather Tom Pats died at the age of seventy-one in 1922. I was only about two years old, so I really didn't know him. My father was eighty-five when he died in 1968. I think my family lived on the island for at least 150 years or maybe more.

I remember my grandmother on my father's side very well. Her name was Máirín Uí Cheárna. She was sometimes called Máirín 'Mhuiris' because her father was Muiris Ó Catháin. We used to call her 'Nan' when we were growing up. She died quite a bit after my grandfather, sometime in the 1940s.

My grandparents had six sons. Three sons lived on the island, Pádraig Tomás, called Pats Tom, Máirtin and my father, Seán Tom. Máirtin never married and lived with my grandparents. They also had three sons who grew up on the island and then emigrated and lived in America, Michael, my namesake, Maurice and Tom.

My mother was from Coumeenole where her family had a small farm. Most of the time, you could see the island in the distance from Coumeenole. It is across the Sound off to the west beyond Dunmore Head. There is gorgeous scenery in Coumeenole; unbelievable.

My mother was one of ten sisters and two brothers. Five of her sisters emigrated to America and five sisters, including herself, stayed in Ireland. She was the only one who got married into the island.

I am a native-born Irish speaker and I love the Irish language. Everybody on the island grew up speaking a pure form of Irish. We also learned a little bit of English in school and even more from the visitors that came to the island. Storytelling was very important on the island. It built a very close-knit community. It was the basis for all the fine literature that came from the island. All my life I have told stories about the island. It is my own way of spreading the word, perpetuating the memory of my beloved island. The island was a place that got into your soul.

Máirín Uí Cheárna – known as Máirín 'Mhuiris' – was Mike Carney's maternal grandmother.

My friend Maurice Guiheen was one of the last people to move from the island to the mainland. He was involved in the final evacuation of the island in 1953. He was a fisherman all his life. Even way up into his eighties, more than fifty years after he moved off the island, Maurice would get up first thing every morning

The island seen from Coumeenole showing Dunmore Head jutting into Blasket Sound. Mike Carney's mother, Neilí Ní Dhálaigh, was born and raised in the house on the right.

and go to the gable end of his new house in Dunquin and look out across Blasket Sound towards the island for a good half hour before he started the day. Maurice never lost his love of the place. He died in 2008, a true islander to the end.

I think that living on the island built strong character. The islanders valued their family and their friends. They relied on themselves and their neighbours. They had tremendous courage and they persevered in the face of great adversity. They used their imagination and made the most out of what they had. They took advantage of opportunities that came up. And they celebrated their language and culture. In my opinion, they were a unique breed of people.

Some people cannot get the island out of their system. I am one of those people. I just can't get the island out of me. I think about it every day and still dream about it at night. I have a love for the island that will never go away. I am an islandman at heart and will be until the day I die.

3. Island Life

I have fond memories of my years growing up on the island during the 1920s and 1930s. They were some of the best years of my life. Even though I left the island at the age of sixteen and a half, I still clearly remember my youth as an islander.

People

The ten main families living on the island were Keane (Ó Catháin), Guiheen (Ó Guithín), Crohan (Ó Criomhthain), Sullivan (Ó Súilleabháin), Daly (Ó Dálaigh), Dunleavy (Ó Duinnshléibhe), O'Shea (Ó Sé), O'Connor (Ó Conchúir), and two separate clans of Carneys (Ó Cearna).

In my time, the Ó Catháins were the most prominent family on the island. Pádraig 'Mickey' Ó Catháin was the King or the 'Rí' of the island. He was not a king in the traditional sense of royalty, but he was the unofficial leader of the island people. He was more like an unelected mayor. The King had the job of going over to the post office in Dunquin by *naomhóg* to get the mail three days a week, if the weather allowed. Ó Catháin was named King because he was a good talker and he had good judgment about things. He was very easy to get along with. My father got on very well with the King. Of course, it always helped to have a good relationship with the King.

After Mickey Ó Catháin died in 1930, the island went without a king. I guess the population was going down and those remaining never got around to naming an official successor. If the islanders needed a spokesperson, the oldest male did the job.

Pádraig 'Mickey' Ó Catháin was the designated King or 'Rí' of the island.

The islanders seldom got into an argument amongst themselves. For the most part, they were able to get along with each other. If they had a problem, it did not last very long. They had no court on the island. They did not need one. They resolved their own disputes. If need be, the King would settle differences using common sense. Afterwards, they would shake hands and that was the end of it.

The King stands second from right, in front of the door. Muiris Ó Catháin, the spokesman when Éamon de Valera visited in 1947, is to his left, with the pipe. This photograph was taken by John Millington Synge in 1905.

The islanders were certainly not wealthy people, but they did not think of themselves as being poor either. Mostly, they were content until they began to realise that their lives might be a lot better if they lived on the mainland or in America.

The women on the island tended to defer to the men on major decisions. The women very rarely went over to the mainland, not even to church.

There was a certain amount of boredom on the island, because we would see and do the same things almost every day. But nobody ever complained, except about the weather.

Nicknames were a big thing on the island, especially among my father's generation. My father's nickname was 'Tooth' because he had an ivory tooth right in front. Other nicknames were: 'Tim', 'Ceaist', 'Léan', 'White', 'Faolí', 'Faeilí', 'Seáisí', 'Buffer' and 'Cuainí'. Nicknames could be either in Irish or English. It was a fun kind of thing to do, but it also helped identify people, because so many people had the same first or last names.

There was not a lot of alcohol on the island, but some of the adults took a drink from time to time. There was certainly never

an alcoholic on the island. An islander couldn't handle it. The conditions were such that they had to be alert and wide awake all the time.

Smoking, on the other hand, was a favourite island pastime. Tobacco was bought in Dingle on shopping trips. Most of the men smoked, and even some of the older women would take a puff or two from a pipe now and again. My uncle Pats Tom smoked a pipe. My father and my uncle Máirtín chewed tobacco. I tried to smoke a pipe, but I couldn't stand it. It wasn't for me.

Islanders were easy-going people. They liked to tell jokes and tease each other. The language used by the men was a bit colourful from time to time. When that happened, the women would just tell them to shut up (*'dún do bhéal'*). And they would. For a while.

But they were also a very shy kind of people, not used to outsiders. And they were always on alert, trying to think of what would happen next, what they were going to do next, and what the weather was going to be and how it would impact things.

Island life required you to be in good physical condition. You had to be 'wiry', as we would say. You had to have manual strength and good bones. For example, you had to be able to help carry a very heavy *naomhóg* down to the ocean and back up to the storage area along the path up from the pier.

Despite all the hardships, I always thought that island life was a fairly happy life. This seems contradictory, but the island people tended to accept things the way they were.

Homes

Most homes on the island were similar to our own. The walls were very thick and made of stones collected on the island. They were mortared with a mixture of sand and cement to seal the gaps and then whitewashed. A fresh coat of whitewash was added almost every year. The roof was black and made of felt that was brought over from Dingle. It would be tarred to prevent leaks and then tarred again almost every year to maintain it in good condition.

The old houses all faced south to avoid the north wind and to catch the sun against the front. Since there was no level ground on the island, the west end of the houses were built into the slope of the hill so that the floors would be level. The houses were very small, usually only a couple of rooms – maybe about 20 by 30 feet on the inside. They had a loft up in the rafters that was used for storage and sometimes as a bedroom. There was a fireplace for heat and for cooking.

Our house had a clay floor that had hardened over time. My mother would sometimes sprinkle fresh white sand from the beach on the dirt floor to give it a cleaner appearance. A few houses had cement floors and some had wooden floors. There was only one door, located in the middle of the front of the house. Some of the doors had two halves so that the top part could stay open to allow sunlight and breezes in. Once in a while, a cow or a donkey would stick their head in the house looking for a handout of some sort. The doors had a latch and bolt to keep them shut during high winds. But there were never any locks. We had no need for locks on the island.

The interior walls were also made of whitewashed stone. There was not much furniture; just the basics. We had a big kitchen table with benches for sitting. We had a wooden tub that was used for a sink. Our mattresses were made from plucked goose or chicken feathers. They were laid on a wooden frame. We hung our clothes on nails in the walls.

Next to the house we had a shed for the animals that we also used as an outhouse. There was a pile of manure outside the shed that we used for fertiliser. Yes, there was some smell, but we were used to it. There was also a small plot of land out in back of the house for grazing our animals and for growing vegetables such as potatoes, carrots, turnip, onions and tomatoes, and some oats. And we grew mangolds, a vegetable like a turnip, for the animals. But the soil was rocky and growing anything was difficult.

The five new houses built by the Congested Districts Board were made of poured concrete with slate roofs. They were white

It was not uncommon for animals to wander in and out of island homes.

and all faced east towards the mainland. They were built higher up on the hill than the other houses and were very well constructed. They were two storeys tall and had three bedrooms. People had to apply for one of the new houses when they were first built. The Congested Districts Board then chose a family from the island that was in need of housing and transferred ownership to them.

Peig Sayers, the famous island author, lived in one of the new houses with her son Micheál Ó Guithín, the island poet. My uncle Pats Tom actually had two of the new houses. He was living in one, and then his brother-in-law died and left him another one. The other two new houses were occupied by Micheál 'Buffer' Ó Catháin and a Seámus Ó Duinnshléibhe; not my godfather, but another man who had the same name.

Five of the Congested Districts Board houses stand at the top of the village. (Two of the buildings are semi-detached).

There was an old stone beehive hut (*clochán*) on the island, just up from the pier by the Dunleavy house. It was a very primitive building originally constructed by monks. It dated way back hundreds of years. But it didn't get much respect. It was used for chickens and donkeys. At one time, they tried to keep ducks in the hut, but they just paddled their way back to the mainland.

Wildlife

There was not a lot of wildlife on the island. The place was just too isolated. There were rabbits, but they were kind of scarce because we used to trap and eat them. My father had a shotgun that he would use to hunt rabbits from time to time. Three other families had shotguns too. Rabbit was very tasty. We would boil it with a piece of pork. It tastes the pretty much the same as lamb or beef.

Island Life

There were plenty of birds on the island: lots of seagulls and some puffins and starlings. There were no trees, so the birds would make their nest holes in ditches or in cliffs or in the roofs of the houses. They'd fly around the island all the time.

There were huge basking sharks in Blasket Sound. They had fins on their backs that stuck right up out of the ocean. And they still live there today. We were under strict orders from our parents to stay away from the sharks; they were big enough to tip a *naomhóg*. But, on the other hand, you never heard of anybody getting attacked by them.

There were only a few seals on the island. The constant movement of the people tended to keep them away. Today, there are lots of seals out there because the place is uninhabited.

Our family had a great yellow dog called 'Róisín', meaning 'little Rose'. A lobster buyer from France, Pierre Trehiou, gave her to us as a little pup. Róisín was very good at catching rabbits. And she was a great family pet. We had another brownish-coloured dog named 'Kerry' that we used primarily for herding our sheep.

Weather

The islanders had great judgment about the weather. They could forecast conditions by looking at the sky and the movements of the ocean, the waves, the currents, and the foam on the rocks, and the direction of the wind. Sometimes you could see rainstorms approaching from miles away. The older people were especially good at predicting the weather. The biggest weather problem was the high wind. The general direction of the wind was from the northeast, but the southeast wind was tough too. The wind often blew like hell, especially in the winter. It would often change direction quickly. The fisherman used to say, 'You've got to go with the wind', because it was impossible to fight it, especially on the open ocean.

The village was tucked in on the island so it was sheltered from the northeast wind by the mainland, and from the west wind by

Heavy winds sweep across the island village in 1897 with smoke from chimney fires being blown by the wind. See the *naomhóg* in the foreground.

the hill on the back of the island. Even so, the wind was so strong it could even blow the roofs right off the houses. The roofs were actually tied down with ropes attached to big stones on both sides of the house to hold them in place.

Sometimes there was light fog and mist early in the morning, especially up the hill on the top of the island. But the fog didn't last very long, because the conditions were so windy.

As a result of the high winds, the ocean was often very rough. Sometimes you would have waves that were 6 or 8 feet high. I remember being at the top of the pier and watching a *naomhóg* crossing the Sound from Dunquin in high winds and waves. One minute you could see the *naomhóg* and the next minute you couldn't because it was down between the waves. It was treacherous out there.

We had a lot of rain on the island, especially in the winter. Heavy showers would be blown by the wind right across the face of the island. We would get soaking wet in about two seconds.

Island Life

It was never really cold on the island, even in the winter. We seldom had snow and, when we did, it was always very light. We would have hail once in a long while. It would pelt down hard, but then melt right away.

Winter days were very short, only about eight to ten hours long. It was very grey and gloomy. Because the village was located in a kind of a natural bowl, the sun didn't shine directly on the houses from the end of October to St Bridget's Day, 1 February. After that date, there was more sunlight and the weather would slowly improve until the summer arrived around 1 May. In the summer, it didn't get dark until about ten o'clock at night. The wind was pretty calm too. They used to say, 'The day was so calm, you could almost walk on the ocean.' The summer ended in the middle of October or so.

The weather was always the subject of conversation among the islanders, especially in the winter when it was bad most of the time. We'd talk about it constantly.

Daily Routine

We would get up first thing in the morning – bright and early – and look out at the ocean and the sky to judge the weather for the day. Our roosters would serve as our alarm clock. One would crow and then all the others would join in. There was no way you could sleep through that racket.

We would wash up quickly every morning. But the men would shave only once a week, on Saturday, so that they would be ready for church on Sunday. They used a straight razor and a bucket of hot water. We never took a real bath. We would just go down to the beach or the pier and wash our whole body with salt water. People gave each other haircuts whenever one was needed.

Most houses had a clock for keeping track of the time. A few people carried a watch. But we also kept track of time by watching the changing position of the sun in the sky.

We all had our own chores around the house. We had to cut or dig turf in a bog at the top of the island. Turf, or peat, was burned

(*L–r*) Ó Conchúir and Seán 'Pats Tom' Ó Cearna with donkeys and creels carry turf back to the village.

in the fireplace for heat and cooking. We cut turf mostly up at the Fort because it was a shorter round trip than the Crow. It was quite a long walk with a donkey, a good mile and a half up to the top of the hill and then back after gathering your load. We never liked that particular chore; it was too much hard work.

Turf was cut with a sharp spade and left up there in stacks to dry in the open air for a month or so. Then it was brought home in a basket or 'creel', one on each side of the donkey. Turf was stored in a 'rick' outside the house until it was used. Towards the end of life on the island, we were actually beginning to run out of turf. The islanders just dug too much of it over the years. The turf burned pretty well in the fireplace, but it wasn't as hot as a coal fire. It smouldered rather than burned. We used to buy some coal in Dingle and mix it with turf to get a better fire.

Cousin Siobhán 'Pats Tom' Ní Chearna and visitor Robin Flower's son Patrick sit at the American Well – see the kitten on the well. The 'Dáil' is in the background.

We had to get our drinking water from wells fed by natural freshwater springs. The wells sometimes ran in a kind of a trickle, especially in the summer. So it often took a long time to fill your pail. That, of course, led to lots of conversation while we waited.

The main well was at the top of the village. It was called 'the American Well' (*Tobar an Phuncáin*) because the women used to talk about America up there all the time. The other well was at the bottom of the village, down next to the Ó Duinnshléibhe house, just above the pier. It was called the 'Well of the Cross' (*Tobar na Croise*), I suppose because it was near the graveyard. It was located on a cliff and you had to be very careful getting out there. Because of the risk involved, it wasn't used very much.

We washed our clothes in the salt water down by the rocks with soap we bought in Dingle. They were rinsed with fresh water from the small stream that ran through the gully.

We kept our animals around and sometimes even inside the house. We had hens walking in and out of the house all the time. We had a half-door, but we seldom closed it. Once in a while, somebody would throw the hens a piece of bread and they'd squawk like mad. When they'd drop their 'stuff' on the floor, the old women would curse them: '*Mallacht na gcearc ort!*' Inside the shed we had a chicken coop with a rooster or two. We had to keep it stocked with fresh straw for laying eggs.

We had to feed our cows and donkeys hay and oats grown on the island and then let them out in the morning to graze. And we had to clean up after them, of course. We had a fenced-in plot of land behind the house for grazing our two cows. Since the fence was too low in places, we had to keep an eye on them to make sure they did not wander onto anybody else's property. We would have to sit there on the wall in the field for an hour or two and let the cows fill themselves with grass. It was like babysitting for cows. This was a regular job for me. I didn't mind it because it was easy and I would bring books with me and read or study.

Winter was a lazy time of year. Days were short and pretty dark. The men went fishing for mackerel and herring if the weather was good. Otherwise, people would go from house to house, listening to stories and playing games. Sometimes, just for fun, the young fellows would go out on the '*Gob*', a point of land jutting out into the Sound. It's named after a bird's beak. There were always strong southwest winds out there; they blew like a hurricane. You would

Mike Carney's paternal grandmother, Máirín 'Mhuiris' Uí Cheárna, sits at her spinning wheel with Mike's cousin Pádraig 'Paddy' Ó Catháin.

almost get blown off the rocks by the wind from all across the whole bay. The lads used to have a regular competition out there on the *Gob*. We would see who could pee the furthest against the wind. No lie. Sometimes, if a gale came up, it would come back in your face. We'd get some of our own right back in our faces! It was a harmless pastime.

The people that lived on the mainland thought that the islanders were a different breed altogether; kind of wildish, I suppose. Maybe it was because of the way they talked. They spoke slightly different Irish than on the mainland. It was hard to understand sometimes. And maybe it was because of the way they walked. When islanders went over to the mainland, we always used to walk along the road following one another, rather than side by side. It was like wild geese, walking in single file. I think it was a habit from walking

on the narrow paths on the island where there was not enough room to walk side by side. The people from the mainland didn't understand it. They thought it was peculiar. When the men used to walk to Ballyferriter for a couple of pints of Guinness after church on Sunday at St Gobnet's, the locals would see them walking in single file along the road and say, 'Ah, the islanders are headed to Ballyferriter.' They knew who they were from a distance by the way they walked.

Every once in a while, the walk to Ballyferriter was not necessary. The parish priest, Father Thomas Moriarty, called 'Father Tom' by his parishioners, had the only car in the whole area. Sometimes he would give the islanders a lift to the pub in Ballyferriter after Mass. The ride was a real treat for the islanders. They loved the novelty of it. But Father Tom wasn't really happy about the situation. He thought that the islanders should be giving their extra money to the Church rather than spending it in a pub.

Food

In my day, we usually had plenty of food on the island. People were healthy. We had to be, because there was no doctor or nurse to care for us if we got sick. We had a good diet – three meals a day. Almost everything was home-made. We would buy our flour in 20 lb sacks in Dingle. We had great fresh baked bread every day. We didn't have too much pastry except for pies and cakes once in a while. I used to love the strawberry, blackberry and raspberry jam and the marmalade that came from Dingle. A piece of fresh baked bread and jam was a meal in itself.

For breakfast, we would mostly have soft-boiled eggs, laid by our hens, with some bread and tea. Sometimes we had porridge or fresh mackerel cooked on tongs over the fire. Lunch was milk and a sandwich. Supper was usually a potato or two with meat or fresh fish. Potatoes were a very important food all over Ireland. My father used to throw a big bag of hot home-grown potatoes on the table. They had been cooked in the oven over the open fire. We would have vegetables as well and, of course, milk to drink.

Blasket women gather 'shore food' in the 1920s.

We ate mackerel primarily in the winter as well as herring and goat fish. And we had pollock, hake and cod too. We had fresh fish in the summer and mostly salted fish in the winter. We used to salt the fish in a small storage room attached to the house and then we would put the fish out on the roof of the house. The sun would harden it up. This would cure it and it could be eaten later. I never cared for salted fish too much. It did not agree with my system. I have a sensitive stomach, like my father. We ate a lot of mackerel, an oily fish. When you cooked them on the tongs in the fireplace, drops of oil fell into the fire and it flared up.

Once in a while, I would go back up on the hill and snare rabbits. I would set the snares at night on the little paths where the rabbits used to run. Then we had nice fresh rabbit to eat the next day.

We didn't eat much meat on the island and when we did it was a treat. Sometimes we had bacon or half a pig's head from Dingle. We would buy a whole side of pre-cured bacon and hang it in the loft on hooks above the fireplace. That would smoke it to improve its taste.

Dillisk, a type of seaweed, was an island specialty. There was plenty of it available. It doesn't sound appetising, but we would

let it dry in the sun on the roof and then chew it like a snack. After chewing for a while, we would spit it out. It was very salty, naturally, and made you thirsty.

Years later, when we visited West Kerry, my brothers and I would bring some seaweed back home in our suitcases so we could enjoy a taste of the island right here in America. It is a good thing the United States Customs officer didn't check our bags!

Another kind of a snack was periwinkles, the little snails. We would gather them up at the shore and boil them in a pot. Then we would pluck the meat out of the shell with a pin and eat them. They were very tasty, something like oysters. We also used them for bait sometimes.

We had our own cows to produce milk and butter. The milk, of course, was unprocessed. There was no such thing as pasteurisation or homogenisation on the island. We had no ice and no refrigeration. Food that would spoil had to be consumed right away. So we chilled it as best we could in the coolest place in the house, usually in a dark corner of the kitchen.

Periodically, we had to bring our cows over to Dunquin, 3 miles across the open ocean, in order to be serviced by the bull owned by the Fitzgerald family who ran the small store located there. We had to tie the poor cow's legs together and put her down on her side in the *naomhóg* for transport over the Sound to the mainland. We had to try to keep the cow calm or she would tip the *naomhóg* right over. We also had to take a second *naomhóg* with us as a backup in case there was an accident. It was a full day's operation with the loading at one end and the unloading at the other. It took a lot of brute strength. One time, a restless cow put her horn right through the side of a *naomhóg* and salt water started pouring in. This was a big problem because most people on the island did not know how to swim. One of the lads quickly took off his cap and jammed it in the hole to stop the water from coming in. That saved the day for all on board. It just goes to show you that the islanders had to be quick-thinking to deal with all kinds of unexpected situations.

Because all this transporting of cows back and forth to Dunquin was so dangerous, the islanders decided to get their own bull on

Islanders have loaded a cow into a naomhóg for transport with a second naomhóg as backup in case of a mishap.

the island. My uncle Pats Tom was in charge of the operation. They went to see a butcher in Dingle named John Moore, and he helped them to apply to the Kerry County Council for a bull.

Lo and behold, they were awarded a bull free of charge. Then, of course, they brought the bull over to the island in a *naomhóg* using the same process as for transporting cows. The bull had big metal ring in its nose that was used to lead it around by a leash. When the bull was done servicing the cows, they brought him over to the nearby island of Beginish to graze. The idea was to keep him away from the cows for a while. Well, that old bull turned up right back on the island the very next morning. Apparently, he could hear the cows mooing on the island in the night. So he swam back to the island, about a quarter mile of open ocean in the dark of night. I still don't know how he did it. I suppose he was highly motivated!

After a while, the bull became too much of a nuisance, so the islanders decided to butcher him for the meat. The four strongest and bravest men on the island got the job. They hit him over the head with a sledgehammer to bring him down and then drove a long sharp knife into his heart. I didn't like it one bit and stayed away from the whole thing.

Sometimes we ate seagull eggs that we gathered on the island of Beginish. We had to test the raw eggs before eating them by putting them in water. If the egg floated on top of the water, we didn't eat it because there was a baby seagull inside. But if it sank to the bottom, it was okay to eat. These eggs tasted very fishy and I didn't like them very much. You had to be careful stealing seagull eggs, or the gulls would swoop down and peck you with their beaks, right in the head. You had to be quick or you'd have a huge headache.

Once in a while, a family would run out of something like sugar, flour or tea. Naturally, you would borrow what you needed from your neighbour. The policy on the island was that as soon as you got your groceries from Dunquin or Dingle, you would immediately return the borrowed item to your neighbour. Nobody wanted to owe anything to anybody.

Clothing

We took great pride in our appearance. The men wore a flat cap that was knitted on the island, or bought in Dingle, or sometimes handed down. The men were almost never without their cap. We also wore a knitted sweater or jersey, a '*geansai*' as we used to call it. When we were young, we wore short trousers down to our knees; they were called 'plus fours' or 'knickers'. The women and girls sometimes wore home-made dresses. But they primarily wore clothes sent over from America by relatives. The older women often wore dark shawls around the head, neck and shoulders to keep them warm and to protect them from the wind.

We were always barefooted when we were children, even in the winter. I got my first pair of shoes when I was twelve. Our feet got

hardened to the ground. But sometimes we'd stub a toe on a stone. The cure was to rub your sore toe with salt water to make it feel better.

We had oilskin jackets that we put on while fishing when it was raining. We bought them from the Frenchman who bought our lobsters and sold us fishing gear.

My grandmother, Máirín 'Mhuiris' Uí Cheárna, had a spinning wheel for converting wool to yarn. The women used to knit things like wool sweaters or jerseys. They would also make socks and caps. They were mostly made for the islanders, but sometimes they would sell them to visitors to make some extra money.

Religion

The people on the island were all Catholic and were very religious. The Protestant Church tried to convert the islanders in the mid-1800s, but without much success. Our parents taught us our prayers and we said them faithfully every night. We had catechism lessons in school in the afternoon. Unfortunately, there was no church on the island. The men of the island used to go to Mass on Sunday in Dunquin when the weather permitted. They would go over maybe once or twice a month, mostly in the summer. If they couldn't go to Mass on a particular Sunday, the islanders would say the rosary together at noon up in Peig Sayers' house.

The parish priest from Ballyferriter came to the island once a year on a set day during the summer to say Mass in the school. Of course, the school was owned by the Church. We called his annual visit 'the Stations', named after the Stations of the Cross. When he visited, the priest would hear confessions, say Mass, give Communion and preach a sermon.

One of the island families would have to provide a meal for the priest when he made his visit. We had the priest eat at our house a couple of times. It was always a special occasion for the Carney family. I was an altar boy in them days, along with my brother Paddy. Mass was always said in Latin. It was '*Dominus vobiscum. Et*

cum spiritu tuo.' We had to memorise it all. We used to serve Mass when we had visiting priests on the island. The priest used to give us a couple of shillings for our effort.

The priests always brought a couple of bottles of altar wine with them. Of course, once in a while, we used to sneak a taste of the wine. We said to each other, 'If the priests are drinking it, I suppose we can drink it too.' It was devilment more than anything else.

All the houses had a statue of the Blessed Virgin Mary. When people eventually moved off the island, they always took the statue with them to their new house. It was a keepsake of the island.

In the summer, we sometimes had priests who would come to visit the island from all over Ireland on holiday. They were looking to improve their knowledge of Irish. These priests had special permission to say Mass on the island. The older women used to love to go to Mass when it was held on the island. It was a big event.

There was a small cemetery at the bottom of the village called 'Castle Point' (*Rinn an Chaisleáin)* or 'the children's burial ground'. This cemetery had not been blessed by the Church and no adults could be buried there. It was only for unbaptised infants and for victims of the shipwrecks that happened over the years off the island. Adults were buried in St Gobnet's cemetery over in Dunquin, called the 'Village Graveyard'.

My father was a very religious man. He used to give me a good slap for swearing sometimes. I suppose I deserved it. I always thought that faith was important on the island because it helped you through the tough times. And there were plenty of tough times.

Health and Medicine

If someone was seriously sick, they had to go off the island for help from a nurse or a doctor. We had the usual childhood ailments like chicken pox, but your parents took care of you and you got over it. It was no big deal. We had a lot of home cures on the island that were passed down from generation to generation.

For sore bones or arthritis, we'd boil water and fill a rubber hot-water bottle and put it in our bed. It would heat your bones and

Parishioners, including islanders, gather at St Gobnet's Church in Dunquin on a Sunday in 1938.

you'd feel much better the following day. Another treatment was to rub your bones with seal oil. For a fever, we put a heated sack of flour on our forehead. If we had digestive problems, we would drink a tea made from nettles.

If you had a bad cold, you might get a shot of hot whiskey with sugar in it to make you sleep at night. My father used to have a bottle of brandy in the house in case anybody got sick. It was French brandy, the good stuff. It was great medicine. If there was something wrong with your bowels, you would drink salt water or '*sleaidí*', an awful-tasting drink made from seaweed. Either one would really get you going.

On those few times when the doctor came to the island, it was big news and the story was told and retold for a whole month. We talked about getting the doctor, and getting him to the island and back to the mainland, and what he said and did. It was all the subject of lots of conversation.

One time when I was a boy, I was running down the hill as fast as I could. I stumbled and fell down and broke my leg. It hurt like hell! My father knew just what to do. He took me by *naomhóg* across the Sound to Dunquin and then by a borrowed donkey and cart to Coumeenole. A local farmer named Micheál Caomhánach was the local bonesetter (*fear cnámh*) for the area. He had learned his trade by trial and error, I suppose. Anyway, he put the bone right back in place. There was no such thing as anaesthetic. More pain . . . And then it was back to the island. I eventually got over it.

There was never a dentist on the island. My father functioned as a kind of a dentist, I suppose. If somebody had a bad tooth, my father would pull it out with a pair of pliers. Or if one of the children needed to have a tooth out, he would tie some fishing line around the tooth and the other end of the line to the door and he would make you run in the opposite direction. Sure enough, the tooth always popped right out.

Transportation

The only way to move around on the island was on foot or by donkey. We did a lot of walking. There was a whole network of narrow footpaths (*cosáin*) all over the island. They led every which way. The main road was improved by the Kerry County Council around 1940. This road was wider than the old paths and helped the islanders to transport the animals, and the turf and other stuff. It led from the pier up to the top of the village and beyond. It was called the 'Road of the Dead' (*Bóithrín na Marbh*) because it went by the seldom-used island cemetery and it was also the road that coffins travelled on the way down to the pier for transport to Dunquin for burial.

The only way for islanders to get from the island to the mainland and back was by *naomhóg*, or currach. It was also used for fishing. Sometimes it was fitted with a mast and a sail, but mostly it was rowed. *Naomhóg* means 'young saint' in Irish. I suppose the idea

was to ask for the protection of young saints from the dangers on the ocean.

A *naomhóg* was made of black canvas stretched over a frame of wooden ribs. There were three or four seats, and each *naomhóg* could carry as many as eight people. They were great around the rocks, because you could manoeuvre them easily with the oars. My father was a good oarsman. He had a very steady stroke. He also made his own *naomhóga*. It required a lot of skill. My brother Maurice could build them too. I didn't even try. It was just not my thing.

The *naomhóga* were stored upside down on wooden support frames set up on the sides of the road leading up to the village from the pier. This would dry out the skin in the sun and wind. They were very heavy and had to be carried up from the water by at least a couple of men. In fact, a couple of men carrying a *naomhóg* over their heads became a kind of a symbol for the island.

It took about forty-five minutes to an hour to row across the Sound between the island and the mainland, depending on the weather. Of course, if the wind and the waves were up too high, you couldn't even attempt a crossing. Then you were stuck until better weather arrived. You needed to be at least thirteen or fourteen years old to handle a *naomhóg*. We used to practise when we were children. We used to try it on our own down by the pier on the island, when there was nobody watching us. I wasn't much of a rower.

Getting the *naomhóg* in and out of the island was a scary proposition. There is a big rock on the right-hand side as you come into the cove by the pier. The movement of the ocean would toss you about as you were trying to land on the slipway. In my estimation, that rock should have been blown up out of there a long time ago. I suppose nobody had the money to do so. And the pier over in Dunquin with its steep and winding access road was not much better.

Nobody on the island had a motorboat in my time there. Towards the end of life on the island, however, Tom and Pat Daly bought

Rocks and calm water frame a view of three islanders with a *naomhóg*. Tom Daly is squatting in the middle. A *naomhóg*, or currach, was a standard form of ocean-going transportation all around Ireland. There are many different designs for these canoe-type vessels that are essentially local in origin. The structure of a *naomhóg* was complex and building them required great skill.

a small motorboat. They owned the island of Inishvickillane and needed the boat to get out there to take care of the place. I often thought that if we had motorboats in my day that the island might still be inhabited today.

Economy

Fishing was the main business of the island. There was a big market for mackerel and other fish in Dingle. The fishing was best in the summer because of the better weather. The mackerel season is in the spring and the autumn. Winter was tough for fishing because there was too much wind, the waves were rough and the days were short.

The islanders fished from their *naomhóga*. They used fishing rods and nets with shell crab for bait. Lines were weighted down with a stone. The catch included lots of different fish like mackerel, herring, pollock, cod, haddock and ling. The islanders were very smart about their fishing. They knew just where to be when the tide turned.

Since they caught fish in relatively small nets, it took a long time to catch enough fish to justify bringing them to market in Dingle. As time went on, the islanders were out-fished by the big engine-driven fishing boats from the mainland, and from places like Britain and Spain. Those boats used large fishing nets and caught hundreds of fish at a time.

Once or twice a year, the island fishermen used to go way out on the ocean near Tearaght and Inishtooskert in a couple of *naomhóga* and go '*spiléar*' (long-line) fishing. It was always during the night because they felt they would get the biggest catch when the fish were feeding at night. But, of course, the darkness made it more dangerous. They would use two boats and set a line between them with a dozen or more hooks with bait. They would let the line down on the very bottom of the ocean and leave it there for an hour or so. Then they would pull the line up and have a load of big deep-sea fish like hake and ray and haddock, and cod – beautiful cod – and pollock. They were big fish, about 10 to 20 lb each.

The fish would always be filleted on the *naomhóg* immediately after they were caught. The guts would be thrown overboard into the ocean. The gulls loved the feast it would create. My father taught me how to fillet a fish properly. But my brother Maurice was better at it than me.

After catching fish, the islanders somehow had to get them to market in Dingle to sell them. There were two choices. You could row your *naomhóg* all the way to Dingle, or you could row to Dunquin and then borrow a horse and cart for the trip to Dingle. Neither way was quick or easy.

In the summer, of course, the main business was lobster. It was a cash crop. We never ate the lobster ourselves because it was too valuable. There was a lobster buyer from France, named Pierre

Trehiou, who came to the island every year in his big motorboat to buy the catch. The islanders stored their lobsters in good-sized lobster pots down near the pier until he came around. Trehiou had a wooden leg as a result of a wound from the First World War. He had a lot of energy and could manoeuvre around his boat like a young fella. He was a jolly kind of fella.

Trehiou visited the island about every two weeks in the summer. We would see him coming in his motorboat around the coast of the mainland beyond Slea Head. His arrival always involved great excitement. He would pay for the lobsters in cash, but he also brought lots of fishing equipment and supplies like lines, nets, hooks and salt for sale to the islanders. His boat was like a floating hardware and fishing supply store. The islanders invested a lot of their hard-earned money in equipment purchased from him.

Trehiou spoke only broken English just like us. He spoke a few words in Irish, but not much. So communicating with each other was a problem. He had a big tank in the hold of his boat where he would store all the lobsters. At the end of the season, he would sail back to France with a boatload of lobsters and sell them to restaurants and hotels.

One autumn, the bay got infested with crawfish because we had unusually warm weather that particular year. The islanders made quite a bit of money selling them crawfish to our French friend. It was an unexpected boon. The fishermen always hated the crabs that lived in the ocean, because they would get into the lobster pots and steal our bait. And there was no market for crab in them days. So we used to take the crabs and whack them against the gunwales on the *naomhóga* to break their backs to make sure they didn't get any more of our bait. But times change, and today crab is sometimes worth even more than lobster.

I used to do a little fishing off the rocks when I was a boy. We'd throw a line out into the ocean with a crab for bait. It was a regular pastime. Sometimes we used a gaffe, like a spear, to catch mackerel. We'd stick it in them and grab them. Once in a while, the mackerel would shoal on the beach and we would scoop them up with a net. Then we had fresh mackerel for supper.

The fishing business was always a topic of conversation on the island. The decline of fishing was part of the decline of the island. There were too many people fishing and prices went way down. After a while, you could not make a decent living at it. Towards the end of life on the island, fishing had declined so much that lobster became the main catch.

Islanders also raised sheep that would graze high up on the hill. At one time, there were about 600 sheep on the island. My father had seventy or eighty sheep that he would graze up there. We had to go and check on them from time to time. Our sheepdog Kerry would herd them for us. The sheep all had a special paint mark on them right in the wool behind the horn or on the neck or the back. Every family had its own designated colour. My family's official colour was green. Sometimes they would put a clip on the ear with an initial, or put a special notch in the sheep's ear to mark it. My father insisted that he could identify his sheep just by seeing them; the build of them and the look of them. I think he was right. He knew each one of them very well.

We would shear the wool from the sheep once a year, on a day in June. I always looked forward to it, because the children would get a day off from school to help out with the job. The sheep would be herded up and brought down to a gravel area at the back of the strand called '*tráigh ghearraí*'. The adults would shear the sheep with hand clippers. The children had to pick up the wool and put it in bags. The sheep were always a lot skinnier and a lot lighter at the end of the day. The wool would be washed in the salt water and then sold in Dingle. Some would be kept on the island for spinning yarn for knitting clothes.

The islanders would castrate their young lambs on the same day as the shearing. This would fatten them up for market, so that good money could be got for them later on. John Moore, the butcher in Dingle, bought sheep that were raised on the island. My father worked for Moore on a regular basis.

My father would cast his eye around and pick out the best sheep from all the owners on the island. With our sheepdog, he would herd the sheep he selected to a grassy area down near the strand.

The island knitting crew. Standing (*l–r*) Máire Ní Dhónaill, the instructor, Bríd Ní Chatháin, Siobhán Ní Chearna, Cáit Ní Chonchúir, Máire Ní Shúilleabháin; sitting (*l–r*) Máire Ní Ghuithín, Cáit Ní Ghuithín and cousin Eibhlín Ní Chearna.

Then he would tie their legs and put them in a *naomhóg* and take them to Beginish for a month or two. Moore owned Beginish and he used it for the final fattening because it was very grassy. Once a month, Moore would come with a motorboat and move his sheep from Beginish to Dingle for slaughter. Working for Moore was good steady income for my father.

Whether it was fishing or raising sheep, the islanders approached work on a shared basis. They had to rely on each other to get all the work done and they split up the proceeds in some way that was fair to everybody involved. Maybe that's one of the reasons why the islanders got along so well. You couldn't carry a grudge, because you would need others to help you with the daily work of the island. Cooperation was a necessary way of life.

The only other kind of business we had on the island was knitting socks. In 1938, the year after I left the island, the government set up a small workshop that involved women knitting socks for sale on the mainland. Ten knitting machines were sent into the island with an instructor. The idea was that if the women were in business, they would be more likely to stay on the island.

But the knitting lasted only about four years before the government shut it down. When the workshop was closed, the government relocated my first cousin, Eileen Kearney (Eiblín Ní Chearna), my uncle Pats Tom's daughter, from the island to work for the government on a similar workshop project in Dublin. She was only sixteen years old at the time.

Islanders conducted their business in cash: with paper money and coins. They certainly didn't have bank accounts. Instead, every family had a safe in its house where they kept their money. It was a trunk, a wooden box with a lock and a key. Other valuables and liquor were kept in there too. There was never any theft on the island. That would have been a sin.

Communications

When Mickey Ó Catháin, the King, would go to the post office on the mainland for mail, everybody would ask, 'What's the news today, Rí?' when he returned. If there was anything going on around the country, the islanders wanted to know about it. What were the big issues of the day? What was going to be done about them?

The King would bring back old newspapers, whatever was left around in the post office. Sometimes they had *The Irish Press,* the *Irish Independent,* or *The Kerryman.* We would spread the news around on the island as soon as it arrived. There was a thirst for information. But, of course, it was always old news by the time it got to the island.

The mail coming from America always involved great anti-cipation. At Christmas, people used to get letters and parcels from

Seán 'An Rí' Ó Catháin, the King's son, arrives with the mail at *Caladh an Oileáin*, the island pier. Seán took over the mail duty after his father's passing.

their relatives in America. By the end of the day, everybody knew what everybody had got. Sharing this information was a favourite island pastime.

In the evening, people would read letters from America out loud for everybody to hear. But the first thing they would do is hold the letter up to a kerosene lamp to see if there was any money inside. Sometimes their relatives would send American dollars. That was cause for great joy!

In 1941, the islanders applied to the government to get a wireless radio system so that they could communicate with the mainland in case of emergency. The radio was battery-powered because there was no electricity on the island. It was operated on the island by another Ó Cearna family, no relation.

The radio was connected to the post office radio system in Dunquin. The radio would ring. Then its handle would be cranked up by the operator and the message would be relayed along with any news. But the radio went haywire all the time. As a matter of fact,

it seemed to be out of order more than it was working. It always seemed to be out whenever the weather was bad. So whenever the islanders really needed the radio the most, it was typically out. This lack of reliable radio communications was eventually a big factor in the island's downfall.

Sports and Games

Our favourite sport on the island was Gaelic football. We played on the strand by the shore. We actually didn't even have a ball. We used a sock and filled it up with grass. We tied it at both ends and then kicked it around.

The two teams were always made up of players from the top of the village and the bottom of the village. I lived in the middle of the village, so we used to flip a coin or cast a stone to decide which team would get me. They were tough, spirited games. I liked to play Gaelic football. I was big and strong and had a physique that was well suited to the sport.

One time, my aunt Bridget Daly Carney, originally from Coumeenole, sent us a brand-new rubber ball from America. That ball was great. It was much better than a stuffed sock. We'd kick it all around on the strand. I remember that, one day, I kicked that rubber ball right through the school window. It broke the glass, bounced off the back wall of the school and came right back out the hole in the glass. It was a miracle. I got my ears pinned back for that one.

And, of course, we had races from one end of the beach to the other and high-jump contests. It was good, healthy exercise.

Once in a while, we used to have a tug-of-war on the strand. We had six or eight lads on each end of the rope. Again, it was the top of the village versus the bottom of the village. Each team had a captain who would pick his team. Who had broad shoulders and good weight?

We would also have wrestling and boxing matches to see who was the strongest or the best fighter. I was a pretty good fighter, but I

Island children frolic on the strand. Mike Carney is second from left.

didn't like it very much. These games were hard-fought contests. We sometimes got mad at each other. But after it was over, that was it.

Sometimes we played a card game called 'high-low-jack'. You had to make your bid in a particular suit to score. If you did not make your bid, your score went down. It was great fun. I played it in America, too, where we call the game 'pitch'.

We played other games like chequers, marbles and ring toss or 'loops'. We also played a game called '*puiríní*' with five pebbles where you would aim and try to hit one out of a circle. And, of course, we played hide-and-seek.

When we were little, we would build sandcastles down on the strand and draw outlines of houses and *naomhóga* in the fresh sand.

We also played a game with mussel shells. We would each get a shell from the beach and fill it with water. Then we'd place it in the cow field where there were lots of flies because of the dung. We would pretend that the flies were lobsters and see how many we

could catch in our shell. The person with the most 'lobsters' won. It was great fun. It was a pastime, but we always maintained that it qualified you to be a lobsterman when you came of age.

Holidays

At special times of the year, like Christmas or Easter, the islanders would kill a lamb with good meat on it, one of the castrated ones. It was like a feast. And we would also have enough to eat for quite a while. I did not like to see my father killing the lamb. In fact, I hated to see him doing it. I had pity for the poor lamb. He would tie the lamb's legs and then quickly slit its throat with a sharp knife. He would let the blood drain in a pail. Later, the blood would be used to make black pudding, a delicacy.

At Christmas time, we decorated the houses with holly, ivy and paper chains. We had a candle burning in every window. It was quite magical. We hung up our Christmas stockings by the fireplace in our house. We'd get an apple or two, or maybe an orange, in our stocking in the morning.

One year, I got it into my mind that I would beat the rest of the family to my stocking, right after Santa Claus came. So, in the middle of the night, I snuck over to the fireplace and got up on a chair to grab my stocking.

All of a sudden, my father opened his bedroom door in his white nightgown. I thought it was Santa Claus! My father yelled, '*Fág ansan é*!' – 'Leave it there.' I was so scared, I fell right off the chair and down on the floor with a big thud. I actually dislocated my shoulder. My father said 'Good enough for ye.' I got no sympathy at all. My shoulder healed by itself.

We always had a big game of Gaelic football down on the strand on Christmas Day. Later in the day, of course, we would sit down and have a big Christmas feast of lamb and bacon with potatoes and vegetables. It was a big family celebration.

On the day after Christmas, St Stephen's Day, we celebrated 'Wren Boys' Day' or the 'Wren' (*Lá an Dreoilín*). You dressed up

(*L–r*) Cousins Eibhlín and Máire Ní Chearna, (later Sr Mary Clemens, SP) and
Tomás Ó Cearna (unrelated).

in a home-made costume and painted your face. You would go
from house to house and people would give you a sweet or a coin.
Then you'd go home and count your haul.

The 'wren' is a little bird, the '*dreoilín*'. It was very hard to catch;
impossible. It is a small brown bird and very fast. They usually came
around at that time of year, so that's why they named the event the
'Wren'.

Weddings

Lots of weddings were scheduled on Shrove Tuesday, the day before
Ash Wednesday. That's because in them days, Catholics couldn't get
married during Lent. It wasn't unusual to have six or seven weddings
in St Vincent's Church in Ballyferriter on the same day.

Islanders sometimes married another islander. But it was hard
to find a mate on the island that was not too closely related. This
problem got worse as the population went down. It also seemed

that there were fewer eligible women than men on the island. There just weren't enough women for the number of men.

So, in my time, most of the weddings involved an islander and somebody from the mainland.

The older people sometimes made a marriage 'match' between a young male and a young female. Or sometimes they would meet at a wedding and the next thing you know, there was another wedding scheduled.

After the service at St Vincent's, the family and friends would go to a local pub for a couple of drinks. They would sing a song and maybe have a set dance or two. Then it was back to the island. Weddings did not involve a huge celebration like they do today. There was no such thing as a honeymoon.

Wakes and Funerals

When somebody died in a small close-knit community like the island's, it was a big event. It was the talk of the island. It was always a big loss, because everybody was pretty friendly with the person that died. After a death, a group of men would be sent to Dingle to get a coffin. A carpenter named Mike Boland, a relation of mine, made all the coffins. They were built of wood with metal handles.

The island wakes were held in the house of the deceased. The midwife or specially trained women on the island prepared bodies for wakes; the lamenting women (*mná caointe*), they called them. There was no embalming. Bodies were dressed either in their best clothes or a long brown gown that looked like a religious habit. They used whatever they had at the time. The body was laid out in the bedroom with rosary beads around the hands. They used to hang white sheets from the ceiling in the bedroom for decoration and to remind you of the heavens, I suppose. They used to burn candles too.

Wakes lasted two nights. We had a keg of Guinness and some wine and they passed around a clay pipe for smoking tobacco. We would eat '*builín*', a type of white bread served with jam.

The people shook their heads and felt sorry about the loss. They prayed the rosary over and over. And the women used to 'keen', or weep, with shawls over their heads. They were crying out loudly, lamenting (*ologón*), and it would go on all night long.

The men were always looking for things to talk about at a wake. They would talk all about the dead person, of course. They would tell stories about the deceased's life on the island. They were just passing the awkward time. At wakes, the old men used to tell me to take a puff of the tobacco from the clay pipe. But I used to hate it. It tasted terrible and it would knock you out. With all the porter or Guinness and wine, you were then ready for some much needed sleep before the morning came around.

On the third day, weather permitting, everybody would get up in the morning and dress up in their best clothes. The coffin would be carried down to the pier on the shoulders of the pallbearers and placed in a *naomhóg* for transport to the mainland. Everybody would turn out. Then five, six, even seven boats of islanders would go over to Dunquin for the funeral, depending on the weather.

The funerals were held in St Gobnet's Church in Dunquin with the burial in the cemetery next to the church. The people from Dunquin would join the islanders in mourning. Then they had a couple of drinks in Ballyferriter or in Kruger's pub in Dunquin after it opened up. Then it was right back to the island.

Politics

People from the island were not very involved in the Irish political movements. The primary struggle that people on the island were involved in was the day-to-day battle with the weather.

The older people sometimes talked politics in the evening. But I was young when I lived on the island and I wasn't interested in political issues yet.

The islanders were all in support of the total unification of Ireland. My father very much wanted to see all the thirty-two counties of Ireland as one independent country. People used to say,

'England's troubles are Ireland's opportunities.' I used to hear that expression all the time.

Dunquin

Dunmore Head is the closest point to the island on the mainland, only about three-quarters of a mile away. But there are huge cliffs and it is much too steep for a landing area. The closest mainland pier to the island is in the small village of Dunquin at the tip of the Dingle Peninsula, about 3 miles from the island.

The pier in Dunquin (*An Fhaill Mór*) has always been very hazardous. It had a good cement landing place, but the road up from the pier was like walking up Croagh Patrick. It is steep and paved with cobblestones. It is a narrow winding road that bends around and around like a spiral as it climbs the cliff. In my day, Dunquin had a small shop named Fitzgerald's where islanders could buy a few necessities, a post office, and St Gobnet's Church with its cemetery.

Islanders often had relatives living in Dunquin. We all shared a life that revolved around fishing and farming. People in Dunquin went out of their way to be helpful to the islanders whenever they could. And, of course, Dunquin later became the home of Kruger's pub, the westernmost pub in all of Europe.

The famous Maurice 'Kruger' Kavanagh was born and lived in Dunquin. He was quite an adventurer. He went to America where he spent time in the United States Army and in Hollywood as an agent for actors and boxers. He maintained that he dated the great Mae West. He said that he was a bodyguard for Éamon de Valera, when he was Taoiseach, on his official trip to America. He said that he worked as an orderly at Holyoke Hospital near Springfield, Massachusetts.

Of course, we never knew for sure whether any of it was true. It really didn't matter, because it was great storytelling. Kruger had a black leather satchel. One day, he went to a cobbler in Dublin and had his name inscribed on the bag as 'Maurice Kavanagh, MD'.

Spiral pier in Dunquin with The Great Blasket in the distance.

Then he went into Leinster House, right past the security guard and into Dáil Éireann (the Irish parliament, for my American friends). Nobody stopped him because they thought he was a doctor. Kruger had a lot of nerve!

Kruger Kavanagh stands beside the van in which he transported Peig Sayers' body
from Dingle Hospital to St Gobnet's Church for her funeral.

Sometime after I left the island, Kruger started a bar and a
guesthouse in Dunquin, named 'Kruger's', of course. He operated
without a licence for a while but got caught by the government and
then went legit. Brendan Behan, the famous Irish author and one
of my friends when I lived in Dublin, stayed there one time. And,
naturally, Kruger himself was always there telling stories.

There was a man named Tomás 'Boiler' Ó Luíng from Dunquin.
Kruger met Boiler's wife one day and she told him that he was
having problems with his bowels. Kruger got a five-gallon bucket
of salt water and a bicycle pump. He went to Boiler's house and
pumped all that stuff right into him. Boiler didn't stop going for
a week! A couple of days later, Kruger asked Boiler's wife how the
poor man was doing. His wife said he was as clean as a tin whistle.

I knew Kruger a little bit was when I was young and living on
the island. I got to know him better when I was living in Dublin.

Dingle and its natural harbour on a calm day.

Kruger and his great friend Joe Daly, from the Irish Folklore Commission, used to come in to see me in Davy Byrnes pub where I was working.

Kruger was quite a man and he had quite a life. He always had big ideas. But he was also a very kind man. He was very helpful to my father when my mother passed away. The islanders loved to tell and retell stories about Kruger's adventures. He was admired as a kind of a local folk hero.

The academy-award winning film *Ryan's Daughter* was shot in Dunquin in the 1960s. They built a whole film set overlooking the island. It was great for the local people. They got paid for lodging, food, and drink and even for acting in bit parts. Kruger's was packed every night.

Micheál de Mórdha, Director of the Blasket Centre, likes to tell a story about Robert Mitchum, one of the film's stars, driving along a road when his progress was blocked by a local farmer herding his

cattle. Mitchum was mad and yelled, 'Don't you know who I am? I'm Robert Mitchum.'

The farmer yelled back, 'I don't care if you're Robert Emmett. These cows can't go any faster!' When Mitchum got back to his lodging he got a lesson in Irish history, including the life and times of Ireland's famous Robert Emmett.

Dingle

Dingle is the closest good-sized town to the island, about 12 miles from Dunquin. It was primarily a fishing village in them days. Islanders would buy all the things in Dingle that they couldn't get or make on the island. They would take a *naomhóg* across the bay and then walk the whole 12 miles to town or ask a relative or a friend from Dunquin to give them a ride by horse and cart.

Dick Mack's shoe shop and pub in Dingle was one of many establishments with multiple commercial uses. It is sometimes called 'the last pew' because it is directly across the street from the church.

Going shopping in Dingle was an all-day event or longer. You had to get enough supplies for a whole month or more. You would get tea, sugar, flour, and pre-cured pork and bacon, pig's head and pig's knuckle. People also bought coats, shoes and trousers. You would get whole bags of stuff.

There were no pubs on the island, of course, but there were plenty of pubs in Dingle. In fact, there were 52 pubs and only about 700 people. I believe that Dingle had the most public houses in Ireland for the size of the town. In them days, you could get groceries, or maybe hardware or shoes in one end of a pub. And then in the other end of the establishment, there was the bar. It was intermixed – a shop and a bar, like Dick Mack's on Greene Street that is both a bar and a shoe shop, or Foxy John's on Main Street that is a bar, a hardware store and a bicycle shop all together.

My father's cousin, Martin Keane, used to have a public house on Main Street named Keane's. The islanders used to buy food and things there. The more they bought at Keane's, the more drink he gave them. But since they weren't used to it, they couldn't handle it. It was not a pretty sight.

Emigration

The huge Irish emigration to America began in the middle of the 1800s. They say that more than 4 million Irish people emigrated to America over the years. Most of them came from rural areas in Ireland where conditions were very bad, particularly during and just after the Famine.

My grandfather's generation included the first islanders to emigrate to America. His sister Nellie Carney (Neilí Ní Cheárna), my great aunt, was the first Carney to make the big move across the Atlantic to Springfield, Massachusetts, probably in the 1880s. Then, in my father's generation, there were four Carney brothers who emigrated to America. In his day, the process was easy because you could come to America without any papers. America was 'open', as they said. In fact, so many people from West Kerry

Annie Moore from County Cork was the first person admitted to America through the new immigration centre at Ellis Island in New York on 1 January 1892. Over 12 million immigrants passed through the facility. It was phased out and then closed in 1954. This statue, in Cobh, County Cork, honours Annie Moore and her brothers.

emigrated that when I was a kid, we had many more relatives in America than we had in Ireland.

The islanders were attracted to America; by the letters, and the money and the beautiful clothes their relatives sent. And they were impressed by the amount of money they made at their jobs. I knew quite a bit about America from school and from the stories I heard on the island and later in Dublin. When all these great stories came back to the island from people who left for America, the motivation to leave increased. As a result, there was even more emigration in my generation than in my father's time. People thought, 'Why can't we go and do the same thing?'

The main reason for the emigration was that the younger generation of islanders was looking for a better life and more opportunities than the island could provide. They were looking for

a better social life too. When the younger islanders went to the mainland, they had a good time. They could meet boyfriends and girlfriends. Frankly, there just weren't enough young females on the island to entice the young men.

So the young people started to move to the mainland to get jobs and many of them eventually went to America. They seemed to go to America, rather than just to the mainland, because the pay was much better in America. The conditions in America were a lot better than in Ireland in them days. A lot of people in Ireland were on the dole and jobs were scarce.

The night before an islander was to emigrate, we held a so-called 'American Wake'. It was basically a going-away party. Most likely, the person leaving would never be seen again. It was a fine send-off, but it was also a sad occasion for those left behind. Everybody showed up to wish their friend or family member well. There was music and drink, but there was also lots of crying – just like at a real wake.

The next day it was off to America. After the trip to the mainland by *naomhóg*, final goodbyes were said at *Barra an Chlasaigh*, the top of the mountain pass along *An Clasach*, the road from Dunquin to Ventry. This is where those leaving took one last look at the island before setting off on the journey of a lifetime.

Most of the people who emigrated from the island went to Springfield and some to Hartford, Connecticut. Both are about halfway between Boston and New York City. Apparently, the emigrants wanted to live near each other in a new and different place where they really didn't know anybody other than their friends and relations. So they wound up living in only a couple of places.

Some islanders went to England, Canada, and Australia too. After the war, those countries needed young men to replace those that didn't come back. They were short of labour. They were looking for immigrants, and the young islanders were looking for opportunities. The result was that the population on the island steadily diminished over the years. And the people who stayed behind on the island were the older people and the very young. These were the people who were least able to take care of themselves. This trend was not good for the future of the island. The downward spiral was under way.

4. Island Education, Literature and Culture

The island was a great place for learning, storytelling, literature, music and dancing. It was a big part of our way of life. But, most of all, we took great pride in our use of the Irish language.

The Island School

The school on the island was owned and operated by the parish of Ferriter, but funded by the government. Attendance was required.

In 1937, the student body of the island school included seven Carney siblings. Seán is far left with Martin in front of him. Maurice, Billy, Mike and Paddy are in the back row. Maureen is front right. Cousin Máirín Nic Gearailt, the last island teacher, is on the right.

My grandfather, Tom Pats Ó Ceárna, apparently donated a small plot of land to the parish for the construction of the school sometime in the mid-1800s. That explains why the school and our house were right next to each other, pretty much attached. I actually did not know about the donation until recently. Oddly, it was not a part of our family's folklore. The donation was discovered by Dáithí de Mórdha at the Blasket Centre when he was researching island land titles. But now I'm very proud that my family was involved in promoting education on the island even going back a couple of generations.

I used to tell my own children in America that when I was a boy growing up on the island, I had to walk 3 miles to school and 3 miles back home every day – barefoot. I was trying to give them a good example to toughen them up. Well, obviously, I was telling a fib. I got my ears pinned back when my kids went to the island for the first time and saw that the school was almost touching our house. I'll never hear the end of it.

The school on the island had only one room. They put the beginners on the right-hand side of the room and the older kids on the left. The students sat on long benches. There were two teachers, one on each side of the room, each with a blackboard on the front wall. The noise of two classes being held in one room was a bit distracting, but we were used to it.

There were about thirty children attending school when I was there; boys and girls intermixed. We had school all winter. But in the summer, of course, we had a nice long holiday from school.

Our teachers taught us through Irish. They taught Irish, a little English and algebra. I hated algebra. We also had arithmetic, and sentences, and writing, and reading, and speech making. And we had history and world geography, especially American geography.

On the wall there were two big maps, one of Europe and one of America. We were taught all the big cities and rivers in Europe and America. The teacher would ask you to go up to the map and show the class different places in America. I always thought that was great fun. We were always very interested in America. The teachers

spoke about it quite often because all of us had so many relatives there.

My father went to school on the island too. He used to talk about a schoolteacher named Thomas Savage. He was from Tralee, a stocky man. I heard lots of stories from my father about 'Mr Savage'. He was a strict disciplinarian with a stick and a leather whip. He was, of course, trying to make sure that the students behaved themselves. My father thought he went a bit overboard.

In my time, we had a teacher named Nora Ní Shéaghdha from Moorestown (*Paróiste Mórdhach*) on the Dingle Peninsula. She was my schoolteacher for most of my years in the island school. She had just graduated from college when she arrived on the island. Later, she wrote a book called *Thar Bealach Isteach* ('Across the Sound') about island life. Miss Shea taught at the school for at least forty years. She taught me on the island in the early 1930s and then, many decades later, she taught my friend and relation, Micheál Ó Cinnéide, when he was growing up in Moorestown in the 1960s.

Miss Shea used the stick quite often. Sometimes we would pinch the girls and tease them to get them to laugh. Or maybe you weren't paying attention to what she was saying. If she caught you, she would give you a good whack on the knuckles or on the legs.

My first cousin, Máirín Nic Gearailt or 'Minnie Fitz' from Marhin (Márthain), Ballyferriter, was an island teacher for a while. She was the one who got us ready for the Preparatory Examination, the national test for getting into college. I always thought that, unfortunately, our teachers did not really want to be teaching on the island. I thought that they would rather be teaching somewhere else. There was very little social life for them; it was too wild a place and there was lots of bad weather.

The island was sometimes said to have a lack of quality education. But in my time, there were four men from the island appointed to the Garda Síochána, the national police: Muiris Ó Súilleabháin, Pádraig Ó Catháin, Micheál Ó Guithín and Tadhg Ó Conchúir. And there were three islanders appointed schoolteachers: Pádraig

Ó Duinnshléibhe and Máirín Ní Dhuinnshléibhe, a brother and sister, and Cáitlin Ní Chatháin. This was a pretty good showing for an island our size, about 170 people at the peak of the population. So our teachers were obviously pretty good.

I loved to read when I was a boy. I used to read books about history, especially about 'the Troubles'. I read stories about Michael Collins, Arthur Griffith and other leaders of the Easter Rising. And, of course, I read about Fionn mac Cumhaill (Finn McCool), the famous warrior. For me, reading was a great adventure. I remember reading *Don Quixote* by Miguel de Cervantes in Irish.

We had books on the island, but not a real library. We had a few books that our teacher let us borrow from time to time. Visitors to the island used to bring books with them, and they often left them behind for the islanders to read.

Eventually, as the island population dwindled, the number of children attending the island school went down too. My sister Maureen moved in with our aunt and uncle, Máire and Seán Mac Gearailt, in the mainland village of Marhin. She then went to school in Ballyferriter. The island school was closed in 1941 when there were only two students left. One of them was my youngest brother Billy.

At that point, Billy moved to Black Field on the mainland and lived with our cousin, Siobhán Uí Shé, my uncle Pats Tom's daughter, so he could go to school in Ballyferriter. Billy had to walk to school each day, a couple of miles each way. And this time I'm telling the truth!

The closing of the school was another reason why life on the island was coming to an end. When a child reached school-going age, the family had to make arrangements for the child to go to school over on the mainland. That created all kinds of hardships for the island families. It often seemed to be easier for the whole family to move off the island.

Folklore

The islanders were noted for telling stories. It was a very important part of daily life on the island. Stories were handed down from

earlier generations and new ones were made up. There were stories about things that happened on the island and to relatives on the mainland or in America. We also told stories about bad weather, especially the wind or big storms called '*gaoth mhór*'.

Most of the stories were true, but some were fiction. Some were funny. Many taught a lesson. We used to question the storyteller too. There was lots of audience participation. It was lots of fun, great '*craic*'. There were stories about Saint Patrick driving the snakes out of Ireland, about the poet and revolutionary Piaras Feiritéar and his adventures trying to escape the British Army, about the wreck of a ship from the Spanish Armada off the island and the drowning of a Spanish princess, about the warriors Fionn mac Cumhail and Cú Chulainn ('The Hound of Culann').

Sometimes they told ghost stories to entertain and scare the kids. Somebody might see a shadow or an illusion and that would lead to a story about fairies (*sí*) or banshees (*mná sí*). Islanders were very superstitious.

Many nights, we used to go visit the 'Dáil' for stories and a bite to eat. This was a house at the top of the village owned by Máire 'na Dálach' Uí Chearna – no relation. Mary always liked company and her house was the main meeting place for people on the island. It was nicknamed the 'Dáil', because everybody went up there to talk all the time.

We also did a lot of storytelling in winter at different people's houses. Guests brought turf for the fire or a bit of food to be shared with the others. In the summer, the stories would be told outdoors, often down by the pier, overlooking the Sound.

A great storyteller was called a '*seanchaí*'. But everybody got into the act. We went around the group and everybody who had a story spoke up when it came their turn. Naturally, you tried to tell a better story than the others. Storytelling was a pastime, something like watching television in America.

My father was a great storyteller. He told stories about America and Springfield, and the people he met from other countries and his job on the railroad. In fact, it appeared that anybody who went anywhere from the island and returned then became a storyteller.

People were curious about life beyond the island. I suppose that all the great stories of life in America contributed to the desire to emigrate.

The Visitors

A lot of visitors came to the island to study Irish, mostly in the summer. The island was one of the few places where people spoke only Irish and its form of Irish was pure. If you were an Irish scholar, the island was the place to go. It was a kind of an educational holiday in a very beautiful place.

It was always a big deal when the visitors arrived. We could see them coming across the Sound in a *naomhóg* and we always gave them a big welcome. When the visitors landed, we would greet them saying '*Fáilte, a dhuine uasal*'. This was a traditional greeting in them days. The visitors would usually respond with '*Lá breá*' ('fine day'). These were often the only Irish words that they knew. So the islanders started to call the visitors the '*Lá breás*'.

There was no hotel on the island, so the visitors would stay with island families that had extra room. The visitors would pay for their room and board. It was a 'bed and breakfast' type of situation.

The visitors loved to go hiking and swimming. And they loved the storytelling. They usually carried notebooks and they were constantly writing things down.

On nice days, we would take the visitors back up to the top of the hill to the Fort and the Crow and show them the whole island. They would give us a shilling or two for our trouble.

When I was a boy, one of the visitors to the island gave me a shilling for giving him a tour of the island. I hid the shilling under a stone up in the gable in our old house to keep it from my brothers. Then I forgot it. I suppose it's still there!

People on the island used to talk about the visit of John Millington Synge after the turn of the twentieth century. Synge wrote the play *The Playboy of the Western World*, which was based on people he met on the island. Carl Marstrander from Norway was another visitor. He once qualified to be an Olympic pole-

vaulter. People said that one time he jumped right over a house on the island using the oar from a *naomhóg* for a pole. His nickname was '*An Lochlannach*' ('The Viking'). Synge and Marstrander were before my time. In my day, the most important visitors included George Thomson, George Chambers and Kenneth Jackson, all from England.

But the visitor who made the biggest impression on me was Robin Flower. He was a student of Marstrander and a keeper or curator at the British Museum in London. He came back to the island year after year.

Flower's nickname was 'Little Flower' or '*Bláithín*'. When he got married, he spent his honeymoon on the island. He often brought his wife and his family with him. One time he took a leave of absence from his job and spent a whole year on the island with his family. His children even went to school there.

Flower used to sit down with the people and smoke a cigarette. He was interested in learning as much as he could about island life. We would talk in Irish and English intermixed. The islanders felt that Flower had earned the right to be called an islander. He even had his ashes scattered on the island when he died.

We would have long conversations with other visitors in Irish and this would improve their knowledge of the language. And we would listen to the visitors and pick up some English. The learning was a two-way street.

The visitors spent their time primarily with the older people. My teacher told us kids to leave them alone. So we maintained a bit of distance.

Probably the biggest legacy of the visitors was in encouraging some of the islanders to write down their stories and helping them to do so. This was the basis for all the great literature that came from the island.

Island Authors

I think that the sea has some kind of quality to it that makes you able to see things more clearly. There are fewer distractions.

Someone once said, 'if you want to become a good writer, go live on an island'. Maybe that's why the island was home to such a large number of famous storytellers and authors for the small size of the population.

I knew all three of the most famous authors from the island, Tomás Ó Criomhtain (Thomas O'Crohan), Muiris Ó Súilleabháin (Maurice O'Sullivan) and Peig Sayers. They were all great story-tellers. That's how they became great writers. Their books were translated into many languages and have been read around the whole world. I read all the most famous books about the island when I was living in Dublin, including Ó Criomhtain's *The Islandman* (*An tOileánach*) and *Island Cross-Talk* (*Allagar na hInse*), Ó Súilleabháin's *Twenty Years a-Growing* (*Fiche Bliain ag Fás*); and Sayers' *Peig* and *An Old Woman's Reflections* (*Machnamh Seanmhná*). These books were all published in the 1920s and 1930s.

There are now more than fifty books about the island. It seems that the whole story of the island captures the imagination of people everywhere. Through these books, people in Ireland and in America became aware of the island as a very special place.

Tomás Ó Criomhthain

The famous Tomás Ó Criomhthain was born in 1856 and died at seventy-one in early 1937, just before I left the island. I attended his wake. It was a fairly quiet affair with all the usual lamenting.

Ó Criomhthain learned to read and write in Irish in the school on the island. He had some English too. He taught both Marstrander and Flower how to speak Irish during their visits to the island. And, in turn, they encouraged him to write down his life story and his observations on life on the island. These writings became the widely read books *The Islandman* and *Island Cross-Talk*.

Ó Criomhthain had plenty of tragedy in his life. His son Tomás drowned one day in heavy surf down on the strand trying to save

A statue of Tomás Ó Criomhthain stands outside the Blasket Centre.

his sister Cáit and Eibhlín Nic Niocaill, a visitor and the girlfriend of the famous patriot Patrick Pearse. Young Tomás and Eibhlín both drowned.

Actually, my uncle Pats Tom dived right into the water with his clothes and hobnailed boots on and he somehow managed to keep Cáit afloat until a couple of lads in a *naomhóg* were able to pull her out of the water. Only his bravery prevented an even worse tragedy. Pats Tom was awarded a bronze medal by the King of England for his efforts and he always wore it proudly for special occasions.

Anyway, they said Ó Criomhthain was never the same after that very sad event. He was a little lost.

Brian Kelly, a visitor from Killarney, helped Ó Criomhthain to edit his books and a visitor named Patrick Sugrue, nicknamed '*An Seabhac*' (The Hawk), helped to get them published. I knew An Seabhac very well. We both lived on Morehampton Road in

(*L–r*) Robin Flower and Tomás Ó Criomhthain.

Dublin for a while. I would drop in to see him from time to time to talk about the island.

Ó Criomhthain was very old when I was living on the island. I remember visiting his house during the Wren and getting a pinch of sugar from him. For the most part, he was quiet and kept to himself. I think it was just his old age and the hard life he lived.

Ó Criomhthain could see that life on the island was drawing to an end. In the last chapter of *The Islandman* he wrote: 'I have written minutely of much that we did, for it was my wish that somewhere there should be a memorial of it all, and I have done my best to set down the character of the people about me so that

some record of us might live after us, for the like of us will never be again.' These were prophetic words indeed.

Muiris Ó Súilleabháin

Muiris Ó Súilleabháin was about fifteen years older than me and I knew him pretty well. He was born on the island, but his mother died when he was one or two years old. He spent a number of years living in an orphanage in Dingle and moved back to the island when he was maybe eight or nine. He actually had to learn Irish when he came back to the island because he spoke only English on the mainland.

One of the visitors, George Thomson, a professor from King's College in Cambridge, England, became a close friend and mentor for Ó Súilleabháin. Thomson had a serious romance with my cousin Mary Kearney (Máire Ní Chearna). There was even talk of marriage, but Thomson was a Protestant, not a Catholic. Their relationship broke off and Mary later emigrated to America where she became a nun, Sister Mary Clemens, SP. She did a lot of good work for children from broken homes.

After he completed school on the island, Ó Súilleabháin thought about going to America but instead he went into the Garda Síochána. He got his Garda training in Phoenix Park in Dublin. When he came home to the island in his garda uniform and cap, we thought he looked like a general in the army. He had a great physique. I started to think that I might want to be a garda myself. For a time, we all wanted to be in the gardaí, just like him.

Ó Súilleabháin was a great talker. His books were about things that happened on the island while I was growing up: stuff like chasing rabbits, catching birds, and playing in the water on the strand and the devilment we used to do.

Thomson encouraged Ó Súilleabháin to use *The Islandman* as a model and to write about his life up to the point when he joined the gardaí. Ó Súilleabháin was well educated on the island and could read and write in Irish. His book, *Twenty Years a-Growing*, was written with help from Thomson who also helped translate

(*L–r*) Seán Ó Criomhthain, Eiblín Ní Shúilleabháin, unidentified girl, Peig Sayers' son Micheál Ó Guithín, Muiris Ó Súilleabháin (with the accordion) and Mike Carney.

it into English. I really enjoyed *Twenty Years a-Growing* because it was about life on the island at about the same time I was living there. I could easily relate to it.

Thomson and Ó Súilleabháin were close friends for years. Ó Súilleabháin was stationed up in Connemara and later in Galway. He left the Garda Síochána to write full-time, but it didn't work out and he rejoined the police.

Unfortunately, Ó Súilleabháin drowned in Galway Bay just off Salthill in 1950. The word was that he had a heart attack when he was swimming. He was only about forty-five years old. It was yet another tragedy. I read about it in *The Kerryman* when I was living in Springfield. I was shocked, to say the least!

Peig Sayers

Peig Sayers was born in Baile Bhiocáire, Dunquin, and went into the island when she married an islander, Pádraig Ó Guithín. But, like many other island women, Peig kept her maiden name.

(*L–r*) George Thomson from England with Muiris Ó Súilleabháin, shown here in his garda uniform.

Peig was a very, very slow speaker. She was a very articulate woman. She became a great storyteller and she had a wonderful memory – instant memory. She was like a radio within herself. She made a big impression on the visitors.

Peig used to talk about growing old. She said she had one foot in the grave and the other on its edge. This is the very first sentence of her famous autobiography, *Peig*. I don't know how these things came to her. She had a gift for words.

Peig became famous all over Ireland because, for years, her autobiography, *Peig,* was required reading for schoolchildren throughout Ireland. Since Peig couldn't read or write, her son

The gifted storyteller Peig Sayers.

Micheál Ó Guithín helped her with her literature. She essentially dictated her stories to him and he would write them down. Micheál was a poet himself and spent time in America. A visitor named Máire Ní Chinnéide, who I knew in Dublin, edited her work and An Seabhac helped to get her books published.

Peig was a very religious woman. She used to say the rosary at her house on Sundays when we could not get to Mass in Dunquin. We all had to go to say the rosary whether we wanted to or not. The praying went on forever. Oh, my poor knees from the cement floor!

My mother was very friendly with Peig. I suppose it was because they both married into the island from the mainland. They would get together and talk from time to time.

Peig moved off the island in the early 1940s when her health declined. She moved back to her former village of Baile Bhiocáire. She gradually went blind. Her son Micheál and lots of old friends used to visit her in the hospital and read to her. She died in Dingle Hospital in 1958. Because of her fame, her funeral was a big event in West Kerry and was attended by lots of dignitaries.

But, like Ó Criomhthain and Ó Súilleabháin, Peig lives on through her books about the island.

Music and Dance

The islanders loved music. They made their own music by singing or playing the tin whistle, the violin, the melodeon – a small accordion or squeeze box – the mouth organ or harmonica, and the Jew's harp, a metal instrument played by plucking a metal prong held in the mouth.

My father wanted me to play the violin, but I had no time for that kind of thing. I was not interested in music.

The islanders would actually make violins from the 'wreck' (*reac*) wood they collected on the beach; they were very handy people. The Dalys and my brother Maurice used to make violins in the winter when they had the time. They would carve the violin out of the wood and buy a string and a bow in Dingle. These violins may not have been the best quality, but they played beautiful music.

Music was played on our instruments in the evening when the day's work was done or in the winter when days were short. In later years, music would be played on the gramophone, the Victrola. You would wind it up and it would play music. We thought it was a miracle.

The songs on the island were often lamenting songs. They'd be singing something like 'people have gone away; we'll never hear from them any more; we'll never see them again; that's the final word.' It was like crying the blues.

'The Coolin' ('*An Chúilfhionn*') was kind of our national anthem on the island. The story goes that a woman way back

Visitors and islanders dance in the island schoolyard in 1947.

thought she heard another woman lamenting. So they made song of it. It is a sad song or 'keen' played on the violin with harmonicas and the accordion too. It would be played at wakes or when the islanders were remembering someone who had gone away, maybe to America. It was very touching. Another favourite was 'The Faeries' Lament' (*'Port na bPúca'*), yet another song about loss. It was played primarily at wakes.

The laments came down from earlier generations. They included 'Dark Rosaleen' and 'Jimmy Mo Mhíle Stór'. They were all connected with something that happened in the past in Ireland or on the island. They had a historical basis.

We would also do set dances: reels and jigs and hornpipes. People from places like Dunquin, Coumeenole, Moorestown, Ventry and Ballyferriter would come into the island for the weekend to dance. We would dance in the 'Dáil' or in the new houses or down on the strand where there was a level strip of land. We would kick up quite a bit of dust with the furious movement of our feet; often there was actually a cloud of dust. We would spread sand on the floor to keep it down. We always said that our visitors would go home with the

soles of their shoes all worn off from dancing on the cement floors in the new houses.

And, of course, there was also an opportunity for a little romance among the young people. Sometimes boys and girls would wander away up the hill along the paths for a little bit of romantic time together. All this was great *'craic'*. I have fond memories of those times.

5. The Carneys: An Island Family

There were many reasons why islanders decided to move to the mainland or America. They were pretty satisfied with island life, but the truth was that it involved lots of hardship. They heard good things about opportunities in America and they wanted a better life. I maintain that a lot of people on the island were sick and tired of fighting the weather and the ocean all the time, and of a life based on the dwindling fishing business. They wanted to get away from it all.

As time went on and conditions on the island got worse, the pull of the mainland and America got stronger. And then people wanted to avoid being left behind in a bad situation without a mate as others moved away.

My father, Seán Tom Ó Ceárna, grew up on the island and went to school there. He spoke Irish and enough English to get by. He wasn't a big reader or writer. He felt the strong pull of America and emigrated not once, but twice. He stayed for about five or six years each time and then went back to the island for good.

People leaving for America usually took a passenger ship from the port of Cobh in Cork, about a hundred miles east of the island. Tickets were purchased at Galvin's Travel Agency located on John Street in Dingle. The boat fee was only £5. In them days, it was very easy to go to America. No visa or passport was required. There were no security clearances; just up and go. The crowded ships landed in Boston or New York. People had to pass a health inspection and then travel to their final destination from there, usually by train.

The first member of my family to leave for America was my father's aunt, Nellie Carney, who emigrated to Springfield, Massachusetts.

Mike Carney's father, Seán Tom Ó Ceárna, emigrated to America twice but
eventually married and settled down on the island.

She was certainly a very brave woman to come over to a whole new
world all by herself. She paved the way for the rest of us to follow.
While Nellie was courageous, she was also a very quiet woman. She
did domestic work and never married. She kept to herself. She was

eventually followed to Springfield by my uncle Michael Carney, the first of my father's generation to emigrate.

My father was anxious for a change from the island. He wanted a different kind of life. So he thought he would join his brother Michael in America. He was only nineteen at the time. It was just after the turn of the twentieth century. Later, two of my father's other brothers, Maurice and Thomas, went to America. That made four Carney brothers in Springfield, including my father. We always said that they were like wild geese, following one another.

Like so many others, my father went to Springfield on a ship from Cobh to Boston. He stayed with his brother Michael and his wife on Everett Street, near Mercy Hospital.

It was not easy to get jobs when my father first came out to America. At that particular time, jobs were scarce. There was also lots of job discrimination against emigrants from Ireland. There were infamous signs that said 'No Irish Need Apply'. It was not a good situation.

My uncle Michael came up with a plan to get my father a job on the Boston & Albany Railroad. Michael was a 'ganger', a foreman, for the Boston & Albany. There was a man who worked for him who was not very punctual and he used to overdo it with drink over the weekend. One Monday morning, my uncle brought a pint of vodka to work. He said to the man, 'How do you feel this morning?' 'Not too good,' he said. He must have enjoyed himself too much the previous night. So my uncle gave him the vodka bottle and told him to go down the line and take a few swigs of it to get rid of his hangover. Naturally, the man couldn't resist the temptation and drank the whole bottle.

Then the big boss came along and found him drunk and sleeping down along the boxcars. So the boss fired him on the spot. And, just as planned, the big boss immediately hired my father in the new vacancy. As a result of this clever strategy, my father worked for the Boston & Albany for many years. My father always said that working for the railroad was very hard, back-breaking work. But the pay was pretty good for the times, so it was worth the effort.

My father's best friend in those days was an islander named Mike Keane (Micheál Ó Catháin), the son of the King. They had emigrated to America together.

One day, my uncle Michael came home for lunch and his wife announced that my father had gone back to Ireland that very morning. My father all of a sudden upped and went back, simply because his friend Mike Keane had just gone back and he missed him.

My uncle was shocked and even a bit aggravated at the situation. I suppose they went back for sentimental reasons. Keane and my father were both island-sick. Maybe my father didn't want to admit his yearning for the island to his brother after all he had done for him.

But my father found very little work back home on the island except fishing. Then, when Mike Keane went back to America again, my father went back to America with him. And when he got to Springfield, my father went back to work for the railroad. He was fortunate enough to get his old job back. Obviously, my father and Keane were very close friends.

Everything in them days was done on the spur of the moment. That's the way they operated. No hesitation, just take off . . .

Mike Keane used to play a violin out on his front porch on Carew Street, one of the main streets in Springfield. People called him 'The Fiddler'. He played Irish songs and the music for set dances and people walking by would stop and listen. They loved the music, even though they did not understand the words of the songs. Eventually, The Fiddler started a small band and they played Irish music for various events in the Springfield area.

When The Fiddler went back to the island from Springfield, he brought his fiddle home with him. But when he returned to America, for some unknown reason he left it in the attic of a pub on Goat Street in Dingle. About a hundred years later, that same fiddle was discovered and its history was tracked down. It has now been restored to its original beauty by The Fiddler's descendants. It is now on display in the Blasket Centre in Dunquin. It is certainly a very well-travelled instrument with a lot of history to it.

The grandchildren of Mike 'The Fiddler' Keane, great grandchildren of 'The King', in 2007 with the famous fiddle from the island and Springfield. (*L–r*) Jack Kane, Joanne Jacob, Mary Kane and Larry Kane.

After another couple of years of working in America, my father came back to the island for good. This time, he came back because he maintained that he had a stomach problem and the food in America did not agree with him.

My father had some form of a stomach ulcer. He was always complaining of a 'gastrated' stomach. But on the island, the food was home-cooked and it was totally agreeable to my father's stomach. Unfortunately, I think I inherited my father's stomach.

My father got a silver watch from the railroad as a token of appreciation when he went back to the island the second time, a Hamilton watch engraved with his name. He was very proud of it. That watch is now on display at the Blasket Centre.

But the second time my father came home to the island from America, Mike 'The Fiddler' stayed in Springfield for good. The two best friends went their separate ways.

When my father came home he had a new ivory tooth right in the front of his mouth where everybody could see it. It was quite a thing in America in them days. He had some kind of a toothache

and the dentist pulled his tooth and put in an ivory tooth in its place. The islanders got a big kick out of it too. They'd say 'Seán Tom Ó Ceárna is home from America with an ivory tooth!' They even gave him the nickname of 'Tooth.'

It took my father quite a while to settle down. He had tried living in America twice, but he eventually settled and lived most of his life on the island.

Seán Tom Carney and Nellie Daly

A couple of years after my father came back to the island from America for the last time, he got married to a girl named Neilí Ní Dhálaigh from Coumeenole. The wedding was on 2 March 1917, at St Vincent's Church in Ballyferriter. My mother was twenty-one and my father was thirty-five. The difference in their ages was not at all unusual at the time.

The marriage was arranged by my mother's father. I think my father had met my mother once or twice. He might have met her in church or when he was visiting in Coumeenole. But it wasn't like they met in a dance hall and fell madly in love. In fact, I've heard that my mother may have fancied another man from Coumeenole.

It was fairly common for men from the island to get married to women from the mainland. There just weren't that many eligible women on the island. Of course, everybody thought it was great for a girl to marry a man who had been to America. It was quite a thing.

My father was six foot tall, a well-built man. He had a long jaw. He was more of a handyman than a fisherman. He could do anything with his hands. I'd say that he would have made a good carpenter if he went about it. He was a hard worker and a good provider. But in them days, there wasn't much work on the island except for fishing and raising sheep.

My father was tough. He was very strict. If you did not do what you were told, you would pay a good price. He had a leather strap, and a big stick and a strong hand. And I got my share of all three!

Mike Carney stands in front of the building in Coumeenole where his mother was born. It is now a gift shop.

My father was educated on the island. He spoke only Irish on the island, but picked up quite a bit of English while living in America. He was an all-round man. He thought carefully before he said anything. But when he said something, you had better listen. He didn't say much unless you asked him a question. My father was a lamenter, I suppose. He seemed to have lots of regrets.

As for my mother, she was a pretty easy-going woman. She didn't have too much to say either, but she sang to herself all the time. She was a beautiful singer. She was about five foot seven inches tall with a pretty face and dark hair. To tell the truth, I don't believe that my mother ever wanted to go into the island to live. But in those days when a girl got to a certain age, it was time to leave the house. She did not have much choice.

Fortunately, my mother did not have far to go to visit her family back in Coumeenole. She would go over to the mainland to visit her family once in a while and they would come into the island to visit her from time to time. Her family's house in Coumeenole overlooked the Sound and the island. It is still there today and is now used as a gift shop for tourists.

But as I remember my mother talking, I'd say she would rather have stayed on the mainland. She had lots of family there and she missed them very much. My mother's constant singing was a way of lightening her burden, I think. She too had regrets.

The Carney Home

Our family home was in the middle of the village, next to the schoolhouse and was handed down to us from my grandfather. The ownership of the houses was passed down within the family. If the owner passed away, then the oldest son or daughter occupied the house. It was a traditional thing.

My father owned the Carney family home. His older brother, Pats Tom, as the eldest, would normally have inherited the house but he already had a house of his own up on the top of the village. Years earlier, Pats Tom had applied for one of the Congested Districts Board houses from the Kerry County Council. And he got it! So my father got the family house.

I really don't know whether we paid any taxes. The islanders were barely scraping by, so they couldn't afford to pay taxes in any event. The government always seemed to have a battle with the islanders, saying that the residents should pay something on their homesteads. But the islanders maintained that, since they were 3 miles out from the mainland, they were outside of any government jurisdiction. But, of course, the islanders had no problem taking an old-age pension from the government. There was no 3-mile limit on pensions!

Space was pretty tight in our house. We had only a combination kitchen-cum-sitting room and two bedrooms plus the loft. My parents raised a family of nine of us, seven boys and two girls, in that little house. We were overcrowded, to say the least.

At some point, my father put an addition on the house, so we had four rooms. Still, there were four of us sleeping in one bed. If you were the last one to get into bed, you had to sleep across the bottom. Then you were all black and blue in the morning from the pounding of everybody's feet during the night.

Seán Tom Ó Ceárna, Mike Carney's father, stands in front of his house. In the foreground is the school and farther down is the Ó Catháin house.

My father built the addition himself. He got the stones up on the hill or down near the *Gob*, the point of rock that ran out into the ocean, and he built the walls and put a roof on it.

We had an open fireplace where my mother did all the cooking. There was a cast-iron oven in the fireplace where she made fine big cakes, sometimes with raisins. She would put the cake outside on the windowsill to let it cool. When we were children, we used to sneak by and grab a chunk off and eat it. My mother used to chase us all around for doing that.

My mother and father had one bedroom and all the children used the other bedroom. My sister Cáit slept in the loft. You could see the ocean from the window in the loft; it was a beautiful view across the Sound. You could hear the rain and the wind hitting the roof.

One night, the wind blew the roof right off the addition my father built on our house. They called it 'the night of the heavy wind' (*oíche na gaoithe móire*). The wind took the roofs off a lot of the houses that night, even though most of them had ropes and

Neilí Uí Cheárna, Mike Carney's mother, holds his baby sister,
now Maureen Carney Oski.

stones to hold them down. I was only an infant when it happened.
But it was a story that was told and retold in our family many times
over the years.

The Carney Children

We had a big family with ten children. My mother, the poor
woman, had a baby about every year. I think it took a toll on her.
There were mostly big families on the island. Ours was not unusual
in that respect.

My sister Cáit was the oldest of the family. My brother Maurice (Muiris) was second, the oldest of the boys. Then there was me. Next came Paddy (Peaidí), John (Seán), Tom (Tomás), Martin (Máirtín), my sister Maureen (Máirín), and finally Billy (Liam). We also had a brother, James (Seámus), the last to be born, who died at only two months of age. He was buried on the island in the small, unblessed graveyard at the bottom of the village.

Cáit was our leader, an amazing woman. Maurice was about a year older than me. He was a fix-it man. He was handy and used to build *naomhóga*. He wasn't much interested in fishing. But he caught some lobsters from time to time. Maurice was like my father in many ways. He and I were different, but we were very close. I never qualified for that handyman stuff. I was the talker of the family.

Paddy was a nice, quiet fellow, a fisherman. He never got married. He had a delicate stomach, like me and my father. Martin was pretty quiet. He was a good fisherman and handyman. He was very strong and liked to play sports. Seán was usually called 'Seáinín', meaning 'little Seán', to distinguish him from my father. I was closest to Cáit, Maurice, Paddy and Martin. The others were a lot younger than me.

When I was a teenager, I went to Coumeenole and stayed with my mother's family on their farm every year for a couple of weeks or so – until they got tired of me, I suppose. I would help out on the farm, picking potatoes, stacking hay, and tending the sheep. It was a kind of working holiday. There is a beautiful beach in Coumeenole at the bottom of a tall cliff. It has gorgeous white sand bordered by huge black rocks. The waves are huge and people go surfing there today.

Like all youngsters, we got into devilment of all sorts on the island. There was an old woman who lived all alone in the house next door to us, Neilí Ní Chatháin. She used to go up the hill by the Fort to get turf for her fire. While she was away, Maurice and me would sneak into her henhouse and take some of her eggs.

Then Neilí used to complain that her hens were not laying. We used to tell her we had plenty of eggs and we'd sell her some of her

Island boys stand for a photo. Standing (*l–r*) Mike Carney, Muiris Ó Catháin, Thomas Ó Cearna (no relation) and Maurice Guiheen; sitting (*l–r*) Mike's brothers Tom, Martin and Paddy Kearney.

own eggs back for a penny a piece. She was on an old-age pension and she had plenty of pennies.

My family's way of living was very spare. We didn't have money to travel here and there by any means. It was hard living, but we got by and we really didn't know any better anyway.

My Mother's Death

My mother was a happy person, despite the fact that she had no love for the island. She was young when she got married and, sadly, she was young when she passed away. She died on 1 July 1933, at the age of thirty-seven, leaving a husband and nine children. It was the year after the International Eucharistic Congress was held in Dublin.

Once in a while, she mentioned pressure in her chest. She talked about stomach problems too. Some people said she cut herself on a briar while digging turf and got an infection.

My mother was a woman who never wanted to let on that she was sick. She mostly kept it to herself. It was typical. The island people did not complain a lot; they kept things to themselves.

She took sick on the island and they took her to Dingle for treatment, then to Tralee, and then even to Dublin.

She had to go to Tralee and to Dublin by ambulance from Dunquin. It was a huge expense, and my father did not have the money to pay for it. He gave the ambulance bill to the parish priest in Ballyferriter, hoping that he would find a way to help pay it. And the priest gave it right back to him. Then he gave the bill to a visitor to the island, a Protestant minister named Frank Roycroft, who had come to the island to improve his Irish. My father gave it to him to see what he could do about it. And my father never saw the bill again. What a relief!

Anyway, my mother died in Dingle Hospital after receiving the last rites from the priest. I am not sure exactly how she died, whether it was a blood clot or stomach cancer or an infection or something else. My father kept the whole thing within himself. He just did not talk about it.

The night she died, my mother's relatives from Coumeenole lit a signal fire on Dunmore Head over on the mainland to let the islanders know that she had passed away. It was before the wireless was installed on the island. I was only thirteen years old.

Her body came back from the hospital the next day and stayed in St Gobnet's Church in Dunquin overnight. There was no wake. The funeral was the following day and she was buried in the old cemetery, right next to the church. Children were not allowed to go to funerals in them days. I was too young.

I remember clearly the day my mother was buried. I stood on the island and looked across the Sound at the church in Dunquin. It was a beautiful clear and calm summer day. I could see the bright reflection of the sun on the handles on her casket, the poor woman. I cried and cried. Cáit went to the funeral as the oldest of the children. She cried her heart out.

When my father came back home from the funeral, he was heartbroken. His eyes were all red from crying. But he never said too much about it; he always kept it to himself. It was the island way. Unfortunately, he was never the same again.

Cáit Takes Charge

After my mother died, my father and my sister Cáit made an agreement that she would take over the family. Maybe Cáit offered it; I don't know. Something had to be done. But, despite the tough circumstances, all of us turned out all right. In fact, I'd say we did pretty well. Cáit did a fantastic job, the poor woman. She was only sixteen when my mother died. She couldn't further her own education because she had to take care of the rest of us. We were all going to school at the time. Maurice was fourteen. There was me, there was Paddy, there was Seán, there was Tom, there was Martin, there was Maureen, and finally there was Billy who was only about a year old when my mother died.

Seán moved up the hill to live with Tom Pats Carney, my grandfather, my grandmother, Máirín 'Mhuiris', and my uncle Máirtín. He basically grew up in that house. It was a good arrangement for everybody. The rest of us were at home, eight of us.

Cáit was trying her very best to keep us all together. She had to do the washing and the cooking. I don't know how she did it. She was a highly dedicated person. She was a great lover of Irish music and kept up the habit of singing around the house that was started by my mother. She had a beautiful sweet voice.

There are some funny memories too. One time Cáit was complaining about a cat we had. It was wild and was driving her crazy. 'Get rid of that damn cat', Cáit told us.

Maurice and I had a plan. Maurice was the engineer on the job. I was his assistant. Before school the next morning, we got an old canvas sack and put a stone in the bottom of it. Then we put in the cat in the bag, tied the top and threw it in the ocean. It was a big

Cáit Ní Cheárna (later Uí Chearna) flanked by her charges (*l–r*) Tom, Martin, Paddy and Billy – in his bathrobe.

operation. That was the end of the cat. We had done the job and we were pretty proud of ourselves. Then we went to school for the day. But when we came home from school, Cáit asked if we had got rid of the cat. 'Sure,' we said, 'no problem.'

Then Cáit said, 'You did? Well, look for yourself. He's sitting right up there in the loft!'

You know, cats have sharp teeth and that little rascal must have bitten right through the bag. Next time, we put a couple of extra stones in the bag and that finally finished him off.

Coming of Age

My father bought me my first pair of shoes in Dingle when I was twelve years of age. Actually, it was a pair of black hobnail

boots. There were nails on the bottom to catch the ground so you wouldn't slip.

When I got those new shoes, I felt like a grown-up. It was like the story told by Ó Criomhthain in *The Islandman*. I thought that everybody was staring at my feet. The younger fellas laughed at me with my new shoes.

I got my first pair of long trousers a little bit later, finally getting rid of my knickers. When I started wearing long pants, my friends would say, 'Did you see Micheál Ó Ceárna with the long pants?' They loved to tease you. But it was all in good fun.

I remember getting my first suit and shirt and tie in Dingle. It was a navy-blue pin-striped suit. We bought it off a cart on a fair day in Dingle. Once a month, the jobbers would come from all around the country and they would set up stalls. They had sales on clothes and things.

I don't know whether the clothes were any good, but the price was right. I thought I looked like a million pounds in that suit.

My Education

I started going to school at the age of seven and continued until I was fifteen. You went to school on the island up to the eighth grade when you were ready to graduate. We called it 'primary cert.' I graduated in 1936. I always said that I got a 'HTR' degree. It meant it was time for me to 'hit the road'.

My father always said I had a good head on my shoulders. I always did well in school. I used to get called up to the front of the class quite often to do maths problems or to go to the map and point out different places to the class. I read a lot of books and was interested in reading and writing and talking. I was always interested in education and the Irish language and its advancement. It stayed with me all my life.

Of course, we often discussed what we were going to be when we grew up. In them days in Ireland, some boys talked of becoming priests, schoolteachers or members of the Garda. When we saw

people go away and became a success and then come home, we asked, 'Why can't we follow suit?'

I knew that I did not want to be a fisherman, but I thought about becoming a schoolteacher. I wondered, 'Am I going to be a storyteller? Am I going to write a book?'

I took the Preparatory Examination to be a schoolteacher in 1935. I saw this as the best chance to advance myself. You had to sit for the test in Ballyferriter. It took a day or two. You got paid £10 by the government for expenses. My father got the £10, not me.

Even though I passed the test, I wasn't called to go on to teacher training. Apparently, there was an influx of young people from West Kerry who took the exam that year, and a lot of them passed. There were too many qualified and not enough openings. Two of us on the island, myself and my friend Maurice Guiheen, passed the test that particular year but we weren't called. We were out of luck.

If I had been called, I would have gone to boarding school in Ballyvourney (*Baile Mhúirne*) in Cork for a couple of years and then to St Patrick's College in Dublin for another two years to be trained for a teaching job.

In them days, the educational system was controlled by the parish priest. If you didn't take care of the parish priest financially, the parish priest did not take care of you. My family did not have as much money to give to the Church as the farmers and the members of the Garda Síochána and others on the mainland. So when there were not enough slots available, I was out. It's not that way any more, thank God.

You could try the Preparatory Examination again later, but you had to be under the age of fifteen. Unfortunately, I would have been over the age limit the next year. I'm pretty sure that if I had taken it again, I would have been called up. As it was, my formal education was over. But, throughout my life, I never stopped learning. I picked up quite a bit of English from the visitors to the island. I would say that my English was more or less self-taught using my own system. I learned the roots of the language in school and from the visitors.

Then I bought a dictionary and looked up words I didn't know. Then I'd gradually work them into a conversation. And, of course, I practised. It was practise, practise, practise.

Then, when I moved to Dublin, I was around English speakers all the time and I picked it up pretty quickly. I had no choice.

6. From the Great Blasket to Cahersiveen to Dublin

Leaving Home

I was sixteen and a half years old when I left the island in 1937. I was the first one of my immediate family to leave the island. I felt that the Carney family was living on borrowed time with respect to financial support. It was a day-to-day proposition. And frankly, I didn't like fishing, the main business of the island. There was too much hardship in it. You had to be out in the weather, working hard all day and you never knew whether you would catch anything. Too often, you caught very little or nothing at all. It was always a gamble and I did not like the odds.

Actually, I was also afraid that I might drown while fishing. Most islanders spent a good portion of their life on the ocean, but they never learned how to swim. It is hard to believe. I only learned to swim in my twenties when I was living in Dublin.

When I was sixteen, I was ambitious. I wanted to meet girls and go to the dance halls and the cinema. I wanted to be free of the limits of island life. There were just too many constraints on the island.

A school principal named Pádraig Breathnach who lived across Dingle Bay in Cahersiveen *(Cathair Saidhbhín)* used to visit the island every summer with his brother Finnian. The great Irishman Daniel O'Connell, nicknamed 'The Liberator', came from near Cahersiveen. Pádraig's wife passed away at an early age and he had no children. There were four Breathnach brothers: Pádraig, Finnian, Michael and Cormac. They were highly involved in the

movement to bring about the freedom of Ireland. Cormac lived in Dublin.

Pádraig was passionate about Irish. When he came to the island, he hired me as his tour guide and we spoke Irish together. It gave me something to do, and I picked up a couple of shillings. He stayed in my uncle Pats Tom's house on the top of the village.

Pádraig saw that my father was having a hard time making ends meet. He proposed that I move in with him at his home in Cahersiveen. He thought my father and Cáit would have one less mouth to feed and one less youngster to keep an eye on. He told me that he had a house with a small garden and a pony. He had a woman to take care of the house and he said I could help him with his garden.

Pádraig was my mentor, my guidance counsellor. He spoke with my father first, and my father was very pleased with the idea. I suppose my father felt that it would help the family if somebody left the nest.

My father gave me his blessing. He said: 'Whatever you say and whatever you do, Mike, do it right.' He put his hand in his pocket, the poor man, and gave me five shillings. I doubt that he had any more than that five shillings. He blessed me, and put his hand on me. He cried. And so did I.

He also told me, 'Keep your eyes open all the time and keep your mouth shut most of the time.' That is great advice for anyone at any time.

The experience of moving off the island was a real eye-opener for me. Before I left for Cahersiveen, I had been as far away as Dingle only twice in my life. I was in for a huge adventure.

Cahersiveen is located on the south shore of Dingle Bay on the Iveragh Peninsula. My father took me in a *naomhóg* to Dunquin and then in a horse and cart to Dingle. Then we said our sad goodbyes at the train station. There were lots of hugs and tears. I took a train to Tralee, through Killarney and then southwest all around the Ring of Kerry to Cahersiveen. It was a big loop and a long, lonely ride, about a hundred miles. Pádraig paid my train fare.

Pádraig's house was located away from the shore in a small village called Mastergeehy, Irish for 'master of the wind', or 'windy place'. My mentor met me at the train station.

I was bit homesick at first, but I got over it. I took care of Pádraig's pony and the garden, and he paid me two shillings a week. That was the beginning of my long working career.

The only thing I did not like about Mastergeehy was that I could not see the ocean from Pádraig's house. And I was a little lonely at first, because I did not have any friends. Back in the island, I would play sports and have fun with my friends. Now I was by myself most of the time. But I had my very own room and my very own bed. There was nobody to kick me in the head at night. It seemed like a real luxury.

Pádraig made me read history books and books about 'the Troubles'. And he would teach me a little English. But mostly, he wanted to speak Irish with me. I was a kind of handyman for him. I would sow the potatoes and take care of the grounds and such.

After a short time, I got used to my new home. I made new friends. We would go to dances in various houses in the village, set dances. They were nice people, very understanding. Cahersiveen was intermixed with regard to language. Most people spoke English, but some spoke Irish. They were glad to have somebody from the island who spoke the pure Irish of the island. Cahersiveen had a Gaelic football team and I got involved with it. We used to go down to Waterville on the coast to play football games. Sometimes we won. Most of the time we lost. But we always had fun.

I never discussed going to America with Pádraig. In fact, I never even thought about it. America was closed to immigration at that time so it was out of the question. I was just trying to get away from the life of fishing on the island. I got along well in Cahersiveen. I had a nice set-up.

An Unexpected Opportunity

One day, Pádraig's brother Cormac told him about an opening for an apprentice in a bar in Dublin. Pádraig sat me down to talk about

it. I had lived in Cahersiveen only about five months. I always thought of it as a kind of way station. I had a sense that there was something greater yet to come. I certainly did not want to go back to the island. But I needed to get some place bigger where I could get a good week's pay and help out my family on the island a bit.

Cormac was a schoolteacher in Clontarf in Dublin. (He was eventually elected a member of Dáil Éireann and served as Lord Mayor of Dublin in 1949–50.)

Pádraig said that the apprentice job was an opportunity to meet new people, do new things and see more of the world. He encouraged me to move along. He said, 'You can't stay here forever. You don't want to do this all your life. You need to advance yourself.'

I was a little hesitant. I wrote to my sister Cáit and asked her to let my father know what Pádraig had proposed. My father was anxious that I keep on going in terms of pursuing a career. Cáit wrote back and told me that my father was sorry to see me go so far away from home, but that he was glad to see me headed in the right direction. So I decided to see what might come of this job in Dublin. I said, 'Let's go!' It was September 1937.

Pádraig bought me a new suit. He took me to the train station in Cahersiveen and bought me a ticket to Dublin. It was a long ride to Dublin, about 300 miles. It took all day. I was full of doubt that I was making the right move.

Pádraig had arranged for me to be picked up at Kingsbridge Station, now called Heuston Station. P. J. Carroll, the owner of the pub, and his son picked me up in his car. A car! There weren't many cars in all of West Kerry. I loved it.

But when I first arrived in Dublin, I thought I had better go back to the island. I had never seen the likes of it. And I thought Dingle was big! I thought to myself, 'I'll never be able to make it.' The traffic . . . The language barrier . . . The people didn't speak Irish, only English. The cars, the buses, the lights, the shops, the houses, the big buildings . . . everybody in a hurry . . . the way they went about things . . . It was all so different from the island and from Cahersiveen.

The staff of Davy Byrnes pub in 1942, including Mike Carney, second from the right.

Apprenticeship: Malloy's

Being an apprentice in them days was a union job. I had to join the Allied Vintners and Grocers Union. The dues were a shilling a month. I spent three years as an apprentice in Malloy's. I got paid five shillings a week during the first year, ten shillings a week the second year and £1 a week the third year. I gradually moved up the ladder. My living quarters up on the third floor over the bar and my meals were both provided at no charge as part of my compensation.

To me, I was making was big money. I even opened up my very own bank account at the Munster & Leinster Bank. After a couple of years when my earnings went up, I would send some money back home to my father whenever I could.

But it was hard work. My father used to tell me that you've got to be determined in life. So I stuck with it. I usually worked at Malloy's from nine o'clock in the morning until ten at night, six days a week. I would have a break in the middle of the afternoon and I had every fifth Sunday off. I used to envy people who did not work on weekends.

Davy Byrnes pub in 2010.

When I moved to Dublin in 1937, there were a lot of people unemployed and on the dole. The government built roads to put people to work. They even paid for the construction of a better road up the hill back on the island. I was glad to have my apprenticeship to move my career along.

There were four lads working in Malloy's at the time. There was a manager, two other apprentices and a porter, a man who did the cleaning.

The Guinness would come in a big barrel, a hogshead. We had to bottle it in the cellar and put the label on the bottles and put a cork in them. We would leave them alone for a couple of weeks and then they'd be ready to be served to our customers. For the draught beer, we hooked the hogshead up to a pump that brought it up to the counter. We learned how to pour it in a pint glass and put a good head on it. Pouring beer, especially stout, is a fine art in itself!

It was the same way with the whiskey. It would come in big 500-gallon containers called caskets; both Jameson and Powers whiskey. The delivery men used to put the barrel up in a stand. We would add colouring from the chemist, the pharmacist, and it would stay there for settlement and to age.

The English spoken in Dublin was different from what I was used to back in West Kerry. They spoke much faster. I couldn't translate that fast in my mind. One time, when I first went to Dublin and my English still was not very good, the manager of Malloy's asked me to 'go get some ham'. And I went upstairs and came back down with a hammer. I thought the man said 'hammer'. We all got a big laugh out of it.

I completed my tour of duty in Malloy's after three years. My apprenticeship was up. It was time to move on.

Junior Barman: Davy Byrnes

Now I was ready to become a junior barman. I applied for a position at Davy Byrnes, a pub at 21 Duke Street, just off Grafton Street near Trinity College. It was a historic pub in a great location, so I was anxious to work there.

Davy Byrnes was referred to as the 'moral pub' by James Joyce who made the place famous in his novel *Ulysses*. Some people say that it is the greatest book ever written.

When I first went to work at Davy Byrnes, it was owned by Davy's nephew Éamon Boland. They had a room in the back of the bar where the leaders of the 1916 Easter Rising used to meet to formulate their plans. Those in attendance included Michael Collins, Arthur Griffith, Éamon Ceannt, Patrick Pearse, Thomas McDonagh and James Larkin. All their pictures were on the wall. I used to love to sit and read about their exploits. I was about twenty years old at the time.

I spent two years working at Davy Byrnes as a junior barman. I got paid £5 a week. I lived in Carmel House on South Circular Road in digs, a kind of boarding house. I got a room and meals there for about £2 a week. I would commute back and forth to Davy Byrnes on my bike. After work, I would go out to the cinema or to a dance.

One day, Seán 'An Cóta' Caomhánach, brother of the famous Kruger from back in Dunquin, came in to see me at Davy Byrnes. He said, 'Mike! My head! I have nothing left but the sockets of my

eyes.' He explained that he was out drinking the previous night with some fellas from the college until two or three o'clock in the morning. I made him a whiskey sour. It's made from the white of an egg, a dash each of lemon, sugar and angostura bitters, mixed with Irish whiskey and all shaken up together in a big glass. He drank it right down in one big gulp. He stood up and his face got red as a lobster and his body shook all over. He paid me, thanked me and walked right out the door. He said he was as good as new.

Shortly after I arrived at Davy Byrnes, Boland sold the place to the Doran family from Marlborough Street. I thought that the Dorans were a kind of high-falutin' people. Jack Doran was a great lover of horse racing. He used to wear a red carnation in his jacket lapel all the time. After the Dorans bought the place, the staff had to wear a white vest and a bowtie. I thought it was ridiculous.

I was fortunate to meet a lot of famous Dublin artists and writers in Davy Byrnes when they would come in for a drink or two. There was Brendan Behan, the author, and Patrick Kavanagh, the poet. And I met a couple of great painters, including Seán O'Sullivan, Harry Kernoff and Cecil Salkeld, whose painting called *Morning, Noon and Night* is still hanging on the wall of the place.

From the Abbey Theatre, we had Lennox Robinson, one of the producers and directors, and actors Cyril Cusack, Dennis O'Dea and Michael O'Brien. And we had actresses Eileen Crowe and Maureen Delaney. They all had great reputations in the theatre. Sometimes they would come around and be really friendly to me – when they were thirsty and out of money. They'd say 'put it on "tick"', a running tab. After the Dorans bought the place, I had to tell them that there was no more 'tick' or I'd get fired. My friends didn't like the new policy one bit.

The Dorans renovated the place. But I almost cried when I saw what they did to the historic back room. They turned it into a cocktail lounge. I thought it was very unpatriotic of them.

Senior Barman: Hennessey's and Hughes'

After two years at Davy Byrnes I became a senior barman – I was twenty-two years old at the time. That meant that I was qualified

to be a manager and could run the whole bar. They called this job the 'foreman'. Those jobs were posted in the union hall and you applied if you were interested.

I looked at the list of openings and saw a posting for a foreman at Hennessey's pub at the corner of Belmont Avenue and Morehampton Road in Donnybrook in south Dublin. The foreman at Hennessey's was in hospital with tuberculosis. I applied and got the job. This new position paid more money, of course. I was now making £8 a week.

I lived in a digs on Morehampton Road for a couple of months and then moved into a flat on Belmont Avenue. I shared the place with my first cousin, Eileen Kearney, who had been involved in the knitting project back on the island. She had since been moved to Dublin by the government, at the age of sixteen. Her father was my uncle Pats Tom. Eventually, she would emigrate to America.

I was working at Hennessey's for about a year when the man who was out sick came back. He had the right to claim his old job back. But I had plenty of notice of his return, so I started looking for another job. The union posted an opening at Hughes' pub on Dorset Street off O'Connell Street, near Parnell Square in the heart of Dublin. The owner, Martin Hughes, was sick in the hospital or sanitarium, another case of tuberculosis. His wife Helen did not have much knowledge about running the place. I got the job and spent almost four years there.

I had to run the whole business, manage the drink, the money, the employees and sometimes even the customers. This is where I learned how to be a good administrator and to manage people. By the time I left Dublin in 1948, my pay was £8 10p a week. That was very good money in them days.

I moved to new digs at 22 Dargle Road in Drumcondra to be closer to my job at Hughes'. I lived there for about four years.

As time went on, I got over my regret that I had not become a schoolteacher. I got accustomed to it and moved on with my new career. In fact, I was doing better financially than a schoolteacher. My friend Caoimhín Ó Cinnéide from West Kerry used to some

Home from Dublin on vacation in 1942, Mike Carney spends time with cousin
Mairéad Ní Chearna (later Mairéad Kearney Shea).

in to see me at Hughes'. He said, 'Mike Carney, you're a lucky man
that you didn't become a schoolteacher.' The teachers went on
strike in 1947 because they were making only £5 a week, compared
to my £8.

Caoimhín was my second cousin. His grandfather, Micheál Ó
Catháin, came from the island. My grandmother, Máirín 'Mhuiris'
Uí Cheárna, and his mother, Eibhlín Ní Chatháin, were first cousins.
Caoimhín grew up in Moorestown in West Kerry and passed the
Preparatory Exam when he graduated from St Erc's School. From
there, he went to St Patrick's Training College in Drumcondra,

in County Dublin, for teacher training. For a couple of months, Caoimhín stayed with me in my old digs on Morehampton Road back when I was working at Hennessey's.

One time when the schoolteachers were out on strike, they were marching and holding placards up around Parnell Square. In the afternoon, Caoimhín and my other teacher friends would come in to visit me at the pub. Of course, while they were on strike they were getting only about £1 a week from the union. So I took care of them with drink. It was the least I could do to help them out.

Once in a while, I'd go to the dog races in the evening with Caoimhín at Shelbourne Park or Harold's Cross. We cycled on our bikes or took the bus. These tracks were always packed with people hoping to make a few extra quid. There were lots of 'hot tips' flying all around. Well, we certainly didn't make a fortune, but we didn't lose much either. It was great fun.

Hughes' pub was a popular gathering spot for people from West Kerry who would come to Dublin to visit or to support their sports teams. The West Kerry people knew I was working there, and it became a regular hang-out. Murt Kelly, Batt Garvey, Paddy Kennedy and other famous Kerry footballers would often come in for a drink – or more.

One time, Paddy Sheehy from Dunquin came in to see me at Hughes'. He was very upset. His wife Maureen had back problems and was in the Mater Hospital in Dublin. Kerry County Council wanted £50 to pick up his wife and take her back to Dunquin by ambulance. Of course, he was beside himself because he did not have that kind of money.

A friend of mine from Davy Byrnes, Éamon Kissane from north Kerry, was a TD in Dáil Éireann. I called him and told him the story. His secretary took down all the details. After a couple of hours, he called me back. 'Tell your friend', he said, 'that the ambulance will be at the hospital tomorrow morning to take the two of them back to Dunquin. And there'll be no charge.'

I told Sheehy the good news. He put his arms around me and I thought he would squeeze the life out of me. He was crying and

told me: 'Mike Carney, when I see your father, I will tell him all about this. He'll be very proud of you.'

Working in the pub was a pain in the neck sometimes. You had to listen to people complain about everything. You had to answer the phone and talk to the mother or the wife or the girlfriend trying to get their man out of there. They'd always say, 'Don't give him any more drink.'

The last time I was back in Dublin in 2006, I checked with a barman at Davy Byrnes and you don't have to serve your time as an apprentice and a junior barman any more. Now it's just show up and you're hired. It's not like the old days.

Second World War

I lived in Dublin almost eleven years, from 1937 to 1948. The Second World War was fought and won during my stay. I remember the day that Britain declared war on Germany. It was 3 September 1939. It was a dark day indeed. I was walking down O'Connell Street in Dublin that afternoon in a pouring rain with my cousin, Muiris Sé. We were trying to figure out where we would go later that night in search of a good time after work.

It happened to be the day of an All-Ireland Hurling final, between Kilkenny and Cork. Christy Ring played for Cork that day. He was a hell of a hurler, one of the best ever. Naturally, Cork won. I didn't go to the game that day, because I had to work.

Somewhere along O'Connell Street we picked up word of Britain's declaration of war. The last straw was the German invasion of Poland. Neville Chamberlain was the British prime minister at the time. He was very unpopular because of his policy of appeasement with Germany. But soon Chamberlain was out and Winston Churchill was in.

We had air-raid drills in Dublin every couple of weeks during the war. Britain got bombed by the Germans repeatedly, of course. Belfast was bombed too, because Northern Ireland was controlled

by Britain. Actually, Dublin was bombed 'accidentally' one night by the Luftwaffe, the German air force. The Germans claimed they thought it was Belfast in the night sky. Later, Churchill admitted that the British had interfered with the Luftwaffe's radar, resulting in the confusion. Some Dubliners were killed in Fairview near Malloy's where I was staying at the time.

We also had food rationing in Ireland during the war. Certain basic food items got scarce, like flour, eggs, butter and wheat. Ireland was neutral in the war because of the ongoing troubles with Britain. But we did not want to support Germany either. We thought Adolf Hitler was too much of a dictator, especially after he went into Poland and devastated those poor people.

Some young people enlisted in the Irish Army. Even though Ireland was neutral, we had a small army in case there was a need to defend ourselves. When I was an apprentice at Malloy's, the Local Defence Force – *An Fórsa Cosanta Áitiúil* – was looking for volunteers. So I went down and joined up. I had a uniform and went to meetings once a week.

Before the war, the British wanted to occupy some Irish ports to prevent the Germans from using them to launch an attack on Britain. Éamon de Valera, the Taoiseach, was totally against it. De Valera was a great patriot and the founder of the Fianna Fáil party. He refused. He was concerned that if Britain took over the ports, Ireland would become a target for the Germans. But nothing ever came of this British idea.

Jobs were plentiful in Britain during the war. Lots of Irish were making big money there, because the British men were off fighting. My brother Maurice worked there for a while during the war.

One time during the war, a German plane crashed on Inishvickillane, one of the lesser Blasket Islands. The islanders cleaned up the survivors and fed them and healed their wounds. The survivors stayed on the island for a couple of months and were eventually picked up by the Irish Defence Force. Then they were detained in the Curragh Camp, a military base in County Kildare. I always wondered whether the guards taught them any Irish! After

the war, one of the Germans, a man named Willie Krupp, came back to the island to thank the people for their hospitality.

When America came into the war to help save Europe from Hitler, the Irish were pretty openly rooting for the Allies. But, officially, we were still neutral. I felt that Churchill had a cool attitude towards Ireland. And the Irish thought that Churchill was a warmonger. But Churchill was a very good motivational speaker and a good director of military operations. I'd have to say he did a fine job of managing the war.

The war was always the news of the day in Dublin during those years and the topic of everyday conversation in all the pubs. I remember when the Allies invaded Normandy on 6 June 1944. It was big news. We were all excited that the tide of the war was turning. The Allies finally had momentum on their side. When the war ended in 1945 there was a huge celebration all over Dublin. I was working in Hughes' at the time and it was a wild night indeed.

The Irish Language

When I was living in Dublin, I got involved in promoting the Irish language. It was falling into disuse as more and more people spoke English. I joined the Gaelic League (Conradh na Gaeilge) and was a member of its Keating Branch. The League was founded by Douglas Hyde from Frenchpark in County Roscommon, the birthplace of my future bride, Mary Ward.

Originally, the League was dedicated to the preservation of Irish in Ireland, but later it got involved in promoting a free Ireland. They had a parlour at their club in Dublin where you could go to chat in Irish. People would drop in and listen to us *Gaeilgóirí*, Irish speakers, talk and tell stories. We were trying to keep the language alive for future generations.

Everyone said I had great fluency in Irish, probably because I was born into the language on the island. People from Trinity College used to come into Davy Byrnes to talk in Irish with me. I

had a kind of following. It was a big city, but the word travels fast. 'Mike Carney from the Blaskets . . .'

Around 1940, I used to write human interest articles in Irish once in a while for *The Irish Press*. I wrote an article about my holiday back in West Kerry. I also wrote about giving a pint of blood and about cutting turf in Glencree in the Wicklow Mountains outside Dublin. They paid me a couple of guineas for each article. That was good money for the amount of work I put into it.

I worked for an Irish-language newspaper in Dublin, a monthly called *An Glór* (meaning 'The Voice'). I wrote for *The Kerryman* too. I wrote stories in Irish about ordinary things that used to happen in everyday life. They were human-interest stories. I also used to speak in Irish about the island on Raidió Éireann.

Once I saw an advertisement in *An Glór* for a job with the Gaelic League. They were looking for a '*timire*', a person who would travel around the country speaking and teaching Irish. It wasn't a direct government job. It was an offshoot of the government. But it had nothing to do with bartending. I applied for the job out of curiosity and I got invited for an interview where they detailed what the job involved. I'd be down the country going from village to village on a bicycle, having local meetings to promote the advancement of Irish. There was a lot of travel required and the money wasn't as good as what I was making in the pub. So I said to myself, 'I'm not going to take this job. I can't take a step back in my career and be away from the good life in Dublin.'

The Dublin Social Scene

I had a great social life in Dublin with its cinemas, dance halls and so on. There were no Irish music sessions at night in the pubs in those days. The pub was about drinking and conversation. You could get a sandwich, but not a meal. The drinking age in Dublin was twenty-one, but I didn't even drink much before then anyway. I might have had a beer now and again before twenty-one, but that's classified information!

When I officially started drinking in my twenties, I preferred Smithwick's beer. Once in a while I'd have a cognac, the good stuff – Hennessy's. I served quite a lot of Guinness in my day, but I never liked it much myself.

I used to smoke cigarettes at the time. I smoked Irish cigarettes called Sweet Aftons or English cigarettes called Players. Almost everybody smoked, women too. There were also cheap cigarettes we used to smoke, called Woodbines.

I got in the habit of reading the newspaper every day, *The Irish Press* in them days. I wanted to stay up on current events. I have kept up that habit to this very day. I went to see plays at the Abbey Theatre. I saw *The Plough and the Stars* and *The Shadow of a Gunman*, both written by Sean O'Casey. It was great entertainment.

On my days off, I would go to the Phoenix Park and St Stephen's Green, or browse around the National Library of Ireland and the Dublin Institute for Advanced Studies. Dublin had it all.

I even learned how to swim when I was living in Dublin. There was a porter, named Paddy Burns, from Dublin who worked with me in Malloy's. He used to swim almost every day, even in the winter. When he found out I couldn't swim, he told me, 'I'll take you to the Blackrock Baths, you islander, and I'll teach you how to swim.' So he took me to the pool. It was three foot deep on one end and six foot deep on the other end. To my surprise, Paddy threw me right into the pool at the six-foot end. I was thrashing around and almost drowned. But I also learned how to swim pretty quickly. Paddy had quite a laugh about it, but I didn't think it was at all funny at the time.

Gaelic Football

I was a big Gaelic Athletic Association or GAA fan and a huge supporter of Kerry teams, especially in Gaelic football. I moved to Dublin in September 1937 and I saw my first All-Ireland football final in Croke Park the very next month. There were more than 80,000 people in attendance. The game was a replay since the

previous game had ended in a tie. Kerry beat Cavan by a score of 2-11 to 2-6.

A young fellow from Dingle by the name of Tom 'Gega' O'Connor came on as a sub for Kerry and scored a goal. He eventually became one of the best players Kerry ever had. One player, Mike O'Doyle, an insurance man from Kerry, gave one of the Cavan team a broken nose with a big wallop and the referee didn't give a penalty!

Kerry played in an All-Ireland football final at the Polo Grounds in New York City in 1947. This time Cavan won, 2-8 to 2-4. I thought the refereeing was questionable at best.

I'm pretty sure they'll never play an All-Ireland final in America again. It was a bad idea. In my opinion, a game so important to the whole country as an All-Ireland should be played only in Ireland.

I went to about twelve All-Ireland football finals in Croke Park. I saw another fifteen or so finals on television by satellite in America. I went to my last final in person in Croke Park in 1997. It was Kerry against Mayo. Kerry won by three points.

Kerry has won thirty-six All-Ireland championships, so far . . . Kerry's the team that everybody loves to beat. I don't know why they're so good. They must have great feet and great stamina. I know they have great team spirit and great fans.

I did not play much in the way of sports myself when I was living in Dublin. I was too busy working. My job came first.

First Thoughts of Emigration

Dublin was a beautiful city, a very clean city. It was always full of excitement. I used to love to walk down O'Connell Street, one of the widest streets in the whole world. Dublin had crowded pavements and shops and tenements and lots of places to go and cinemas and dance halls. And, of course, there were a lot of pubs. When I went to Dublin in 1937 you were not allowed to spit on the pavement. There was a fine of £5. That's not the case today, unfortunately.

I focused primarily on my work in Dublin. But I was always thinking about the rest of the family back home in the island. I felt that, even though I was not the oldest of the children, I had a certain amount of responsibility since I was the first to leave the island and go to work. I felt my family should be taken care of somehow.

I would write letters home to the island a couple of times a month. So I knew how things were going back there. And the news was not very good. The population was getting older. The complaining was increasing and people were leaving.

When I left for Cahersiveen, I was the first to leave the island. Then my brother Maurice decided to go to England where there was a lot of work during the war, if you could put up with the bombing. Maurice wound up joining the British Merchant Marine and sailed around the world. He went to Canada, to America, through the Suez Canal, and even to Australia.

Then I brought my brother Paddy to Dublin. I got him into the barman's union and found him a job. He was a good-looking, likable fellow. He also liked to sing. But he soon came to me and said, 'Mike, I'm sorry. I am not cut out for this barman work.' He moved to County Meath where he worked on a farm with a man named Michael Long who was originally from Ventry. I brought my sister Maureen to Dublin too. I got her a job in a bed and breakfast near Parnell Square where I knew the owner.

I got a two-week holiday in the summer and would to go back to the island to visit. I stayed in one of the new houses up the hill. I spent a lot of time with my family. But I also went snaring rabbits and hiked up to the Fort and the Crow. I went swimming at the strand, since I was now a swimmer. At night, I might go to a dance hall on the mainland.

I saw that the people on the island were getting too old to manage for themselves. I thought that the government should do something for the islanders before it was too late. As for my own family, I began to think that if I could get a head start in America, then my brothers and sisters could emigrate and move up the ladder in America themselves, every one of them.

So I started to work on a plan to emigrate from Ireland to America. If America did not work out for some reason, I could always go back to Dublin and get my union job back.

In them days, after the Second World War, America had new immigration restrictions. You had to be declared or sponsored by a close relative living in the States: a brother or a sister, an uncle or an aunt, or a cousin. They had to send you the required documentation; the 'affidavit', they called it. This gave you the right to enter the country. I wrote a letter to my uncle Tom Carney in Springfield and asked him if he would be my sponsor.

Mary Ward

One night in 1946, after I closed up Hughes' for the night, I went down to Teachers' Hall, a social club in Parnell Square to dance. A schoolteacher friend of mine, Patrick Cahillane from Comeen in West Kerry, happened to be dancing with this nice girl named Mary Ward. Patrick said to her, 'Here's another Kerryman for you.' She said, 'The place is infested with them! Well, he's another teacher, I suppose?' 'No,' said Patrick, 'he's doing better than a teacher. He's a barman in the pub around the corner.'

A couple of weeks later I got a telegram from a friend of my brother Maurice, a man named Eugene O'Sullivan from England, which said: 'Meet me at the restaurant at Powers Hotel on Kildare Street' on a certain date. On the night our get-together was scheduled, I hopped on my bike and went over to the hotel. I asked the porter if he had a Gene O'Sullivan there. He said 'No, but I have a Father O'Sullivan here. That may be him. He is going back to England tomorrow.' Out came a priest. To my surprise, he was indeed my brother's friend. 'Come on in,' he said, 'I'm having my supper.'

And then the waitress came over to our table . . . Lo and behold, it was none other than Mary Ward. I said to her, 'So this is where you work?' She was very surprised to see me.

I'd say it was love at second sight.

Mary Ward and Mike Carney attend a 'tuxedo dance' in Dublin.

After that, we started dating. We were both about twenty-six. Mary was from Frenchpark, in County Roscommon. Shortly afterwards, I had a chance to go to a 'tuxedo dance' sponsored by the Allied Vintners and Grocer's Union at the Metropole, a beautiful theatre in Dublin. I thought I'd take the Roscommon girl. She had to get a long gown and I rented a tuxedo. We looked great.

It was a terrific night out. It lasted until one o'clock in the morning. We had a group of eight or ten at the table, mostly fellas from the bar and their dates. We danced. Then we took a taxi home.

But not long after that, my brother Seán died back on the island. That was a heartbreaker.

7. The Decline and Evacuation of the Island

Seánín's Passing

My younger brother Seán, or Seáinín, as we called him, died on 9 January 1947, at the age of just twenty-four. His death signalled the end for the island.

Seán got sick just before Christmas in 1946. There was very bad weather on the island with gale-force winds and high waves. He was sick for only a couple of weeks. I got a note in Dublin from my sister Cáit that Seán had the flu. But, in reality, he had something much more serious: meningitis.

The weather worsened and they could not get him to the mainland to see the doctor, and the doctor could not get to the island to see him. The battery-operated telephone provided by the government was not working at the time – again. It had been out for about a week.

Seán had a really bad headache. He thought his head would blow off! Cáit put a heated sack of flour on his head to try to ward off the temperature, but it did no good. He started to vomit too.

After being sick for over two weeks, Seán's condition got worse. Then one day, Cáit found him dead in bed in our house. Since there was no priest, she whispered an Act of Contrition in his ear in case he was still alive. Then she had to tell my father. It was devastating.

A telegram was sent from the post office in Dunquin to my digs at 22 Dargle Road, in Drumcondra. It was waiting for me when I got home after a hard day's work. It said: 'Your brother Seán has passed away. Please come home.'

I couldn't believe it. I was shocked. It really set me back, because it happened so quickly. I had not seen it coming. I immediately took the train from Dublin to Tralee and then the bus from Tralee to Dingle. It took all day and I stayed the night in Dingle with my father's cousin, Martin Keane, before going on to Dunquin by taxi first thing the next morning.

At the time, Maurice was in Australia. Paddy was working in Meath. My sister Maureen was working in Dublin. Liam was going to school on the mainland. Only Cáit, Martin and Tom were at home. I left Dublin so fast, I didn't even tell Paddy and Maureen what had happened.

Seán's body was still in our house on the island, the poor man. He could not be buried in the small graveyard on the island because it was not blessed. And there was no coffin on the island anyway. We needed to get his body to the mainland.

Three young, strong and brave islanders, Seán 'Pats Tom' Ó Cearna, Maidhc 'Léan' Ó Guithín, and Seán 'Faeilí' Ó Catháin, all cousins, fought the fierce ocean in a *naomhóg* to go and fetch a coffin from the mainland. They were the best boatman on the island at the time. The conditions were such that they could easily have drowned. Their great courage was very much appreciated by my family.

After landing in Dunquin, they got a coffin from Dingle but they could not get it back across to the island. The water was just too rough and the weight of the coffin made navigating a *naomhóg* back to the island too much of a risk.

When I got to Dunquin, the islanders were still there waiting for the weather to break. The weather was not good that day, or the following day either. We were all talking about the situation in the post office. Hannah Daly, the woman who ran the post office, mentioned the lifeboat operated by the Royal National Lifeboat Institution on Valentia Island, near Cahersiveen, all the way across Dingle Bay over on the Iveragh Peninsula. I asked her if she could call and ask them to get Seán's body off the island.

Hannah called the lifeboat station to explain the situation and ask for help. Yes, the officer at the lifeboat station said, they would

A 1972 photo of two of the three cousins who crossed the Sound for a coffin for the deceased Seán Ó Ceárna in 1947: Seán 'Faeilí' Ó Catháin (front) and Maidhc 'Léan' Ó Guithín (rear). Not shown is Seán 'Pats Tom' Ó Cearna. The man in the middle is Seán Ó Guithín.

arrive in Dingle that night to pick up the coffin. The lifeboat could not come in or out of Dunquin because its pier was not big enough to handle it. They had to land in Dingle instead.

So we now had to take the coffin back from Dunquin to Dingle. That night, we put the coffin on the lifeboat, the *C&S*, in Dingle harbour. Then we travelled 12 tough miles over the ocean through huge waves to the island.

When we got into the island, poor Seán, I couldn't look at him. He was lying dead on the bed in my father's bedroom. He had been dead for three days. Cáit had cleaned him up, washed his body with soap and water, and dressed him up, but decomposition had already started to set in. Everybody was crying. We put Seán in the coffin and nailed the lid shut. There was no wake; there was no time. The lifeboat was waiting.

We then went back to Dingle on the lifeboat with Seán's body in the coffin. The waves were still high and it was a very rough ride, and my father came with us, the poor man. It was a heartbreaking thing.

When we got to Dingle, the medical people said they had to determine the cause of death. My father told them to write down that the government killed him. He was very angry and so was I. We felt that the government should have installed a better radio system or provided a motorboat – anything to improve the safety of the people living on the island. This was just the kind of situation we warned could happen.

Our family doctor, Dr Patrick Scully was there but, of course, there was nothing he could do. Dr Eilís O'Sullivan, the Kerry County Medical Officer at the time, had to examine the body and make a finding on the cause of death. It took a couple of hours but her finding was that Seán died from meningitis.

Then we had to take the body another 12 miles back to Dunquin where Seán was to be buried. We left the coffin in St Gobnet's Church overnight and that evening we said the rosary for him.

The funeral and burial were held the very next day, four days after Seán died. I was a pallbearer.

My father was there along with the three islanders who came to get the coffin, and our friends and relatives from Dunquin and Coumeenole. Nobody else from the island could get there because the weather was still horrible.

The funeral Mass was said by Father Patrick McAuliffe, the parish priest. Seán was buried next to our mother in the old cemetery next to the church. It was all so sad.

More Sorrow

The time had come to tell my father about my emigration plans. I knew that it would mean even more sorrow for him, but I really could not put it off any more. The time to depart for America was getting close.

My eleven years in Dublin had opened my eyes. My sister and the two brothers who were still living on the island had no jobs and nothing constructive to do. My other brothers and my sister who were elsewhere in Ireland could do better in America too. I knew we would all be better off some place where we could make a good living. I had made up my mind to make the move to try and help them out.

America was open for immigration and jobs there were plentiful. In them days, you could leave one job and start another the next day. So it all came together, the circumstances and the opportunity.

After Seán's burial, we took a taxi to my aunt Joan Shea's house over in Coumeenole. During the journey by taxi, I told my father that I had written to my uncle Tom about emigrating to America. I said that I wanted to give my brothers and sisters the chance to go to America too. I think my father had seen it coming. He said, 'Mike, I don't blame you. You do whatever you think is right. And, whatever you say and whatever you do, make sure you do it right.' It was the same advice he gave me when I went to Cahersiveen. I suppose it was his standard farewell advice. He was highly intelligent in how to lead you and encourage you to do the right thing.

My father said, 'Mike, you always seem to have a good head on your shoulders. I am sure you could stay in Dublin. Just don't do anything that you'll be sorry for.'

This was the second time I said goodbye to my father. It certainly wasn't any easier this time. My father could see that the nest was going to be empty pretty soon. His heart was heavy and so was mine. We both started to cry.

My father had a hard life. He went to America twice and it did not work out for him. He lost his wife when she was only thirty-

seven and had to raise nine kids. He lost two children, Seámus and
Seán. He had Cáit, but he was worried that he would be all alone
at his advanced age. How would he climb up and down the steep
hills on the island?

I was exhausted from the whole terrible ordeal. I stayed in
Dingle that night and went back to Dublin the following day. I
slept soundly all the way back on the train.

My father stayed in Coumeenole with the Sheas for a couple of
days and waited for the weather to calm down; then it was back to
the island for him.

That was the toughest winter they remembered having on the
island. And my brother's death was the toughest thing that had
happened on the island for as far back as people remembered. It
all seemed so senseless. The islanders came to the conclusion that
it was no place for them to live. Essentially, Seán's death and the
circumstances broke the will of the islanders to continue living on
the island. It was time to move on.

When I got back to Dublin, I called the Roscommon girl to
go to the cinema. Afterwards, I told her the sad story about Seán's
death. More crying . . .

Island Desperation

After my brother's death, I felt strongly that the government should
do something about the island. The conditions were bad and getting
worse. The isolation and the lack of reliable communications and
transportation were huge problems. The islanders were vulnerable
in case of emergency. But there was also the decline of the fishing
industry and the difficulty in making a decent living. The population
was dropping fast. Most of the young people had left. Many of the
people still living on the island were just too old to get along on
their own. Family life was disappearing because no women would
marry island men. The situation was getting desperate.

On 26 January 1947, I wrote a letter to the Taoiseach, Éamon de
Valera, describing the tragic circumstances that led to Seán's death.

22, Bóthar Dairgle,
Dromchonrach, Áth-Cliath.
26-1-47.

ROINN AN TAOISIGH

A Thaoisigh,

Táim a' scríobh chughat tar cheann mhuintir Oileán na mBlascaod, an t-Oileán san go bhfuil a chlú agus a cháil i n-áirde ar fuaid an domhain, ar shon a bhfuil déanta aige do aithbheóchaint na Gaedhilge. Tuigtear do mhuintir an Oileáin seo (mo bhaile dúthchais féin) ná fuilid ag fáil cothrom na Féinne ón Rialtas. Coightheas o' shein do fuair mo chearbhráthair féin, Seán O' Cearna, bás ar an Oileán in aois a cheithre bliadhna fiche de. Fuair sé bás agus níor bhféidir leo an doctúir ná an sagart, a thabairt chuige, cé go raibh sé seachtain breoite agus mara mbheadh an bác-sátháil caithfí e chur i roilig an Oileáin gan an sagart. Níl locht ar bith ar mhuintir na h-áite iotaobh an sceíl; cad is féidir leo a dheanamh i ndroch-aimsir le n-a mbáid bheaga.

Ó's rud é go bhfuil an Rialtas go láidir thaobh thiar go aithbheóchaint na Gaedhilge cad fáth ná tugtar seirbhís ceart do'n Oileán Gaedhealach so. Má's maith leis an Rialtas go bhfanfaidh an t-Oileán so beo caithfaidh siad bed freastail a fhailt o Dhaingean Uí Chúise, go mor mhór san Gheimhreadh. An gléas guthain a Bhuanaig an Rialtas idir an Mín-tír agus an t-Oileán, cupla bliadhain o shoir, is cuma ann no as é, mar bíonn sé briste gach tarna lá. Dá mbheadh cábla curtha féin bhfairrge ann an céad lá, ní bheadh oiread airgid caithte leis is atá leis an gléas guthain atá ann i láthair na h-uaire, mar bítear ghá dheisiú gach lá.

Má's doigh leis an Rialtas nach fiú aon airgead do chaitheamh le Oileán na mBlascaod, cad fáth na tugtar beagan talún dóibh ar an Mín-tír? Sin rud a thaithneodh le muintir an Oileáin féin, mar tá sé ro-chruaidh orra maireachtaint ar an Oileán le cupla bliain anuas. Níl aon t-slíghe bheatha aca ann acht iascairseacht agus toisc ná fuil an aimsir bhreágh ag teacht le bliantá anuas, níl aca acht ó'n láimh go dtí an béal, go bhfóiridh Dia orainn. Tá feirmeoirí ar an Mín-tír go bhfuil níos mó ná a gceart dé thalamh aca, da mbeadh cuid dé riartha ar mhuintir an Bhlascaod, beidís ar muin na muice. Ní thuigeann

einne cás mhuintir an Oileáin sin, comh maith is a thuigim-se, duine a rugadh agus a togadh ann. Is mo aiste tá scriobhta agam le blianta go dti páipéir nuadhachta i dtaobh an sceíl, ac tá na blianta ag imtheacht agus gan faic dá dheanamh, foirior.

Má's doigh leis an Rialtas gur fiú feachaint isteach i gcás muintir an Oileáin, ba cheart duine éigin a chur cúcha cun cainnte leo. Duine go mbeidh colas ar a chúram aige agus fós duine a thuigfidh cad ba cheart á dhéanamh do mhuintir an Oileáin gaedhalach so.

Mise le meas
Mícéal Ó Cearna,

Don Taoiseach Uasal,
Éamon de Bhaléra.

Mike Carney's 1947 letter to Éamon de Valera in Irish, in which he suggested that the islanders be relocated to the mainland.

The Decline and Evacuation of the Island

22 Dargle Road
Drumcondra, Dublin
26 January, 1947

Dear Taoiseach,

I am writing to you on behalf of the people of the Blasket Island, that island which is famous the world over as a result of what is has done for the revival of the Irish language. The people of this island (my own native home) believe that they are not getting fair play from the Government. A fortnight ago my own brother, Seán Ó Ceárna, died on the island at the age of 24 years. He died and they were not able to bring the doctor, or the priest, to him, although he had been sick for a week and if it wasn't for the lifeboat he would have had to be buried in the island graveyard without a priest. The local population cannot be found at fault in this; what can they do with their little boats in bad weather.

As the Government greatly supports the revival of the Irish language, why is this Irish Island not given a proper service. If the Government wants this island to remain alive they must procure a service boat from Dingle, especially during winter. The telephone which the Government installed between the mainland and the island a few years ago, is useless, as it is not working every second day. If an undersea cable had been laid at the beginning, less money would have been spent than has been spent on the current telephone, as it is being fixed every day.

If the Government thinks that it is not worth spending any money on the Blasket Island, why don't they be given a small piece of land on the mainland? That would please the islanders themselves, because it has been too difficult for them to live on the island for the past few years. There are no jobs there except fishing, and as the fine weather has not come for years now, they are only living hand to mouth, God help us. There are farmers on the mainland who have more than their fair share of land, if some of it was shared amongst the Blasket people, they would be on the pig's back. No one understands the Blasket people's story as well as I do, someone who was born and raised there. I have written many essays to newspapers though the years about the situation, but the years are going by and nothing is being done, unfortunately.

If the Government thinks it worthwhile to look into the case of the Blasket people, someone should be sent to speak with them. Someone who would know what he was doing and someone who would understand what should be done for the people of this Irish island.

Yours,

Micheál Ó Ceárna,

For Attention of The Honourable
Taoiseach,
Éamon de Valera

This translation of Mike Carney's letter to de Valera spells out the case he made to the Taoiseach for the evacuation of the island. (Translation courtesy of the Blasket Centre)

Unfortunately, I did not get a reply other than an acknowledgement of the receipt of my letter by the Taoiseach. I was disappointed, but not really surprised. All the same, I thought de Valera was a great statesman. Even though he was foreign-born (he was born in New York City, to a Spanish father and a mother from Limerick), he was a huge promoter of Irish, which he spoke fluently.

To keep the pressure up, I also got in touch with Richard Mulcahy, a member of Fine Gael and the TD from Tipperary. He lived in Rathmines. My idea was to approach the problem by appealing to both sides of the political aisle; to the party in power and also to the opposition. At the time, Mulcahy was leader of the opposition party in the Dáil.

At one time, Mulcahy was a general in the Irish army and Minister for Defence, and he would go on to be Minister for Education. I met him once or twice. I could have asked my friend, Éamon Kissane TD, to get involved but Mulcahy had more seniority and had been a cabinet minister so he would have had more political influence. Mulcahy was a great friend of the island, having pressed the government during 1946 about radio communication with the island and about the horrible condition of Dunquin pier.

I had met Mulcahy's daughter several times. She was a dedicated Irish dancer and she used to go back to Dunquin and into the island to dance. She worked in the Government Buildings in Dublin and gave me her father's phone number. I called him shortly after my return to Dublin from my brother's funeral and told him about Seán's death and the hardship and the difficulties of the island. He invited me to his home at Castle Grove to give him the details. I cycled over to his house and spent about an hour with him and detailed the circumstances on the island. He said that he would see what he could do, but he was not specific about his plans. He was very sympathetic.

Then, on 25 February 1947, Mulcahy brought up my brother Seán's death on the floor of the Dáil during question time. He asked the government why the wireless was always out of order and about the lack of adequate pier facilities. Mulcahy asked the Minister

of Industry and Commerce 'if he will cause a tribunal of inquiry to be set up to inquire into, and to report on, the contributory circumstances under which Seán Ó Ceárna, who recently became ill on Oileán mBlascaod, died there after a week's illness, without it being possible to summon or to bring to his aid spiritual or medical assistance'.

The minister responded for the government. He dismissed the problem as the result of a temporary power outage and bad weather. Mulcahy brought the matter up again on 12 March. The Minister for Posts and Telegraphs was forced to provide detailed information on the radio outages. The Minister reported that over the previous fifteen months, radio service was out for eighty-six days, with partial outages on another thirty-eight days. The Minister promised further inquiry. But nothing ever came of it.

A couple of months after Seán died and a month after Mulcahy's questions in the Dáil, the islanders sent de Valera a telegram saying, 'Stormbound distress. Send food. Nothing to eat.' It was signed 'Blaskets'. As a result, the government sent a boat with emergency food in April. The legend has it that there was some strong drink in the boat, too.

The islanders wanted to keep up the pressure. They realised that the old people couldn't manage and the young people had left. They were stuck. They were up against the wall. Apparently, famous Kruger from Dunquin was involved in some way in sending the distress telegram to de Valera. Kruger was a good leader because he was a good talker. He was always stirring the pot. And he wanted to help the islanders.

Evidently, all this eventually made an impression on de Valera and he decided to visit the island in July 1947 to see for himself. My brother Martin and Pats 'Ceaist' Ó Catháin transported de Valera from his boat to the island pier by *naomhóg* and were paid £3 for their effort. A group of islanders met the Taoiseach at the top of the pier. There were about eight or ten of them, including Muiris Ó Catháin, my father and my uncle Pats Tom.

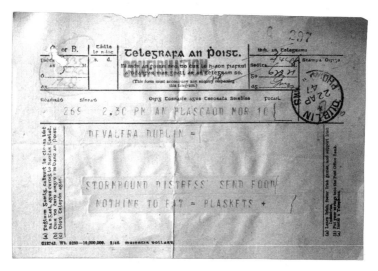

The distress telegram sent by the islanders to de Valera.

The Taoiseach toured the village and talked with the people in Irish and asked questions about their life on the island. He wanted to understand from them directly what the conditions were and whether they wanted to be moved off the island. There had been no King on the island since the passing of 'Mickey' Ó Catháin. The oldest person on the island, Muiris Ó Catháin, was the spokesman for the islanders. He told de Valera that they were suffering great hardship and that they wanted to move to the mainland. They talked about the price of fish and the fact that they had no salt to preserve the fish for the winter.

My father told me that he said to de Valera: 'Get us some place, sir, where we can walk.' What he meant was, get us away from the island and the ocean and move us over to the mainland.

De Valera left the island without making any commitments, but the islanders felt that they had convinced him to do something about the situation. I kept my family up to date on my work in Dublin in support of the evacuation in letters to Cáit. They

Éamon de Valera (right) visits The Great Blasket Island. Mike Carney's father, Seán Tom, is in the middle of the photo scratching his head. Maíre Uí Ghuithín is to the left.

appreciated my effort, but were impatient for results. To them, the hardship seemed to go on forever.

News for Mary

The Second World War ended in 1945, and America opened up for immigration in 1947. There was an announcement about it in the newspapers and a lot of talk about it around Dublin.

I got my affidavit and applied to go to America in 1947, but I was delayed by my brother's death. Then, when that tragic situation

Mary Philomena Ward.

was resolved and I thought that the remaining islanders would be moved to the mainland in the near future, I decided that it was time to move. It was 1948, and it was the beginning of my family's third wave of emigration to America. This time, I was going to lead the way.

I had been dating Mary Ward for about two years. We spent a lot of time together. One night when I walked her home after going to a dance, I said, 'I think I'm going to emigrate to America.' I told her that I was intending to create whole new opportunities for my family.

I liked Dublin a lot. And Mary too. We took advantage of everything that Dublin had to offer. But I was committed to doing something about my family's dire circumstances back on the island. Mary didn't get angry with me. She was easy to get along with, which, I suppose, is why I liked her so much. At the time, based on her reaction, I did not think she would ever emigrate to America and so I had a heavy heart. But I was hoping that she would change her mind at some point.

Six Years of Frustration

After de Valera's visit in the summer of 1947, the islanders had high hopes for a quick resolution of their situation. But they were soon disappointed. The relocation to the mainland did not happen as quickly as they hoped. Governments just don't move very fast. A couple of months after de Valera's visit, the islanders sent the Taoiseach a letter, asking for information on his plan to deal with the situation. In the handwritten note, the islanders said 'if you can't help us, we will have to go across the Atlantic to seek our fortune.' They were trying to raise the stakes. Again, there was no reply.

The last person born on the island was Gearóid Ó Catháin. Born in 1947, Gearóid was called 'the loneliest boy in the world' by *The Irish Press* in 1951. There were no other children because they had all left the island with their families. They said that seagulls were his playmates. It was so sad.

Unfortunately, de Valera was defeated in the elections in early 1948. The future of the island was still up in the air and de Valera's defeat was a blow. The new Taoiseach, Fine Gael's John Costello, did not have much interest in the issue. Over the next couple of

years, there were reports and commissions and inspections related to the future of the island. And I'm sure that there were lots of meetings in Dublin too. But there was no concrete action. In the meantime, the island population continued to decline. The situation was getting desperate as the politicians talked.

Frustration on the island went up. Conditions got worse. It was a vicious circle.

The islanders tried to keep up the pressure. Still another communication was sent to the government in September 1952. There were twenty-eight people still remaining on the island. In a 'memorial,' the islanders pleaded: 'We are prepared for any migration, anything to leave the island, but we will be satisfied with a house and one acre, or even a house, on the mainland.' It was signed by Muiris Ó Guithín, Seán Ó Guithín, Muiris Ó Catháin and Seán Ó Catháin.

With de Valera back in office as Taoiseach, the government decided in late 1952 to evacuate the island; all the remaining islanders were to be moved to the mainland. It was good news at long last and there was some relief in the minds of the islanders.

But the final evacuation of the island was still another year away.

Cáit's New Home on the Mainland

In 1944, my sister Cáit got married to Pádraig 'Sheáisi' or 'Paddy' Ó Cearna, an islander with the same last name, but who was no relation. He was from the other Carney clan on the island. Paddy lived close to our home, just on the other side of the school. He had worked in England for four years before marrying Cáit. After they got married, Cáit and her husband lived in our family's house on the island with my father.

Then Cáit had a baby boy named Seán. At that point, Cáit and Paddy bought a small house in Muiríoch near Ballydavid. Cáit then moved off the island with her family on Easter Sunday in 1948. In the end, my sister Cáit was fed up with the island. She was glad to leave and wasn't lamenting her departure at all. Her patience was

exhausted. She was sick of fighting the wind and the ocean and the circumstances.

My Father's Move to the Mainland

Families were very close back then and took care of their own. People were dedicated to their families; it was a commitment within them. My last two brothers to leave the island were Martin and Tom. Martin had spent time in England, but came home for a time to help out. He then emigrated to America at the age of twenty-one. A short while later, Tom, who had stayed on the island to help my father tend his sheep, also emigrated to America.

At about that time, Cáit then asked my father to move to her house in Muiríoch. My father really had no choice since he was in his late sixties and was too old to function alone on the island. He reluctantly agreed and moved in with Cáit. It was crowded in Cáit's small house since she eventually had five children of her own. So my father built a one-room addition for himself. He had sold his flock of sheep and invested some of the money in the new addition.

In the end, my father wasn't sorry to leave the island either. He was glad to put his feet on the ground, as he said to de Valera. He just packed up everything, left the family home and moved to the mainland. He was the last member of our family to leave the island. The evacuation was still months away. For sentimental reasons, he would visit the island for a month or so during the summer with Cáit's husband and their son Seán.

One day, Cáit's husband Paddy and my father took the roof off the addition on our vacant house on the island and actually moved it to Cáit's house in Muiríoch. They installed that roof on the new addition my father had built for himself. They took it all the way across the ocean to Ballydavid balanced between two *naomhóga*, a distance of about 5 or 6 miles. It was a big adventure! Some people thought they were just trying to save money on a new roof. But they also did it for tradition, for sentimental reasons. It was a

common thing to take a memento from the old house on the island to the mainland. The Ó Criomhthain family did the same thing.

The first thing that deteriorated on the unoccupied stone houses on the island was the roofs. Then, with the homes open to the weather, the deterioration sped up. The result was that the old houses went to ruins over a period of years. Some of the old paths became overgrown with weeds.

My father liked living in Muiríoch. It was a nice seaside village. He still couldn't get away from the ocean. He loved to look out at it. Muiríoch was a fishing village and they had a harbour in nearby Ballydavid with a beach and lobster pots. On a clear day, he could look out from Cáit's house and see the island of Inishtooskert, one of the lesser Blaskets, in the distance. He used to go down to the pier and watch the fishing boats come in. And he would go to Begley's pub or maybe O'Connor's and have his couple of pints and go home. He wasn't much of a pub man. Tomás Ó Criomhthain's son, Seán, a friend of my father's, had moved to Muiríoch too and they spent time together.

Cáit wrote to me in Springfield and told me that my father had moved off the island. Yet again, Cáit had stood up for our family in its hour of need. She was a saint.

For me, his move was bittersweet. I was pleased that, finally, my poor father would be well taken care of in the twilight of his life. No longer did he have to walk up and down the hill on the island and then complain about it to anyone who would listen. On the other hand, our family's long life on the island was over. But I felt that, while there were no more Carneys living on the island, our connection with the island would go on forever.

After our family left the island, there were only twenty or so people still left, the hard core. They could see that the end was near, but they hung on until the bitter end.

The Evacuation

The government's plan for evacuating the island was to entice some of the small property owners in Dunquin to move down

in the country, to the good farming land in Meath and Kildare. Some jumped at it, because it was easier living and more valuable land. After they went, the islanders would move into their former homes in Dunquin or into a few new homes built there by the government. Then the islanders could do their farming and fishing on the mainland. A lot of them were on the old-age pension.

The government evacuated the last of the islanders, beginning on 17 November 1953. Emigration from the island had increased quite a bit since my brother Seán's death six years earlier. The twenty-two islanders left at the end were, as far as I remember:

- Eilís and Seán Ó Cearna – wife and husband – Seán was my first cousin
- Muiris and Seán Ó Guithín – brothers
- Micheál, Pádraig and Seán Ó Súilleabháin – brothers
- Pádraig and Tomás Ó Dálaigh – brothers
- Bríd and Seán Ó Catháin – wife and husband – with their son Gearóid Ó Catháin
- Neilí and Pats Tom Ó Cearna – wife and husband – Pats Tom was my uncle
- Pádraig 'Fíogach' Mistéal – called 'Dogfish'
- Micheál Ó Sé and Máire Ní Shé – brother and sister
- Seán 'Faeilí' Ó Catháin
- Seán 'Sheáisí' Ó Cearna – the brother of my sister Cáit's husband Paddy
- Seán 'Filí' Ó Cearna – a cousin and one of those who went to get the coffin for my brother Seán
- Máire and Seámus Ó Duinnshléibhe – wife and husband

Many of them were up in their sixties – or older. Seven of them were named Seán, a very popular name on the island. There were only three couples, one child and one older single woman. Eleven of them were bachelors in their thirties or forties. They were still single because there were no eligible women on the island and women from the mainland didn't want to marry into the island.

None of my immediate family was left on the island by the time of the evacuation. My brothers and sisters were all off to America. My father and Cáit were in Muiríoch.

On the day of the evacuation, the government sent a fishing boat from Dingle, the *Saint Laurence O'Toole* to pick up the remaining residents of the island and their belongings. The boat was owned by Mike Brosnan from Dingle. It was a typical November day on Blasket Sound with rough seas. This was a challenge because the islanders needed to be transferred from the island to the *Saint Laurence O'Toole* by *naomhóg* which had to make three round trips from the island pier.

Due to the bad weather, only six islanders were moved to the mainland that particular day: Seán 'Sheáisi' Ó Cearna, Seán 'Faeilí' Ó Catháin, Seán Ó Guithín, Seán Ó Súilleabháin, Seán 'Filí' Ó Cearna, and Pádraig 'Fíogach' Mistéal.

The islanders were glad to be leaving. They just loaded a very few possessions on the *Saint Laurence* because of the rough seas and got going to the mainland. The remaining seventeen islanders and the furniture had to wait to be moved to the mainland until the weather improved over the next couple of days. Postal service was discontinued.

There was no ceremony or speechmaking. Not even a drink. They were just glad to get out of there. It took several trips on the *Saint Laurence* over the next couple of days to get the others off the island.

One family, the Sullivans, stayed on the island for about a year after the evacuation. They just refused to leave – for sentimental reasons. But even they eventually moved to Dunquin. At the point of the evacuation there were several times more people from the island and their descendants living in America than there were living on the island itself. The island was pretty much abandoned after that, except for a few people who would go into the island in the summer. Some of the families maintained their homes in good shape for a while and others continued to raise sheep out there. But the village was soon to go to ruin as a result of the harsh weather and lack of maintenance.

The first six islanders to be evacuated are all smiles on their arrival in Dingle. (*L–r*) Seán 'Sheási' Ó Cearna, Pádraig 'Fíogach' Mistéal, Seán Ó Súilleabháin, Seán 'Filí' Ó Cearna, Seán Ó Guithín and Seán 'Faeilí' Ó Catháin. Legend has it that Ó Guithín is carrying an RMS *Lusitania* deckchair that washed up on the island sometime after the ship's sinking off Kinsale by Germany in 1915 with the loss of 1,195 lives.

By the time of the evacuation, I had been living in America for five years. I read an account of the event in *The Kerryman* about a week after it had occurred. I spread the word among the former islanders living on Hungry Hill in Springfield. The reaction was mixed for obvious reasons.

My own feeling was that it was about time. The evacuation did not involve any members of my family, but I was still upset that it took the government so long to act when the only practical course of action was so obvious. I was pleased that my own efforts in support of the evacuation had, at long last, come to fruition but was disappointed not to see it in person. The evacuation was the right thing to do but it had been delayed for too long. Today, there is not much left of the village, just the stone walls from the old houses. And the five 'new' houses that are still in pretty good shape. It's a ghost town, really. And the ghosts are the souls of my forebears. After all these years, the thought of it still nearly makes me cry.

8. Doing All Right in America

When I lived on the island, I liked to visit the houses of families who had relatives who had emigrated to America. I wanted to find out how they were getting on in America. I wanted to know how they went about emigrating, what happened when they got to America and what kind of jobs they got. I was curious about it all. These evening conversations on the island planted a seed in my head. It seemed to me that emigrating to America led to a better way of life.

Although I did not really need to leave Dublin – I had a great girlfriend, a good steady job and no major complaints – I also had a family responsibility. My sister Cáit had stayed on the island with my father. My brother Maurice was serving in the British Merchant Marine. Somebody had to make a move on behalf of the others. I was the third eldest. It was up to me to get the ball rolling. I would be the first in my generation of the family to go and I would get the process started for the others to follow. Dublin was fine, but I thought I could do better and my brothers and sisters could too.

My uncle Tom Carney was one of three of my father's brothers who had emigrated from the island to Springfield, Massachusetts, in the 1920s.

Unlike in my father's day when all you needed was the money for passage on the boat, you now needed lots of documentation to enter America. But emigration was a fairly easy process if you had relatives who were American citizens. You needed an affidavit from your sponsor saying that he or she would be responsible for you for five years after you landed. The affidavit was submitted to

the United States Embassy in Dublin. If you were approved, the Embassy sent you a visa by mail.

In 1946, I wrote to my uncle Tom in Springfield to get my affidavit. His daughter Rita wrote the letters and filled out the forms. A Springfield lawyer named Bill Foley finalised everything. Foley's family was originally from Ventry. I filed my affidavit in 1947. My visa was delivered to me in early 1948. I was very excited and made my travel arrangements right away.

At the time I emigrated, I thought that the evacuation of the island was about to happen at any time. Little did I know that it would not happen for another five whole years.

Arrival in Springfield

I did not tell my employers at Hughes' about my plans to go to America until they were finalised. Helen Hughes was still overseeing the place because her husband, Martin, was still out sick with tuberculosis. When I finally told Helen about my plans, she said she was sorry to hear I was going. But she said that, under the circumstances, helping my family out, she understood.

I had been working at Hughes' for four years. She said, 'If things don't work out, you can always come back here and get your job back.' It was great to have a back-up plan.

Some of my Dublin friends, Stephen Roe, Jimmy Vaughn and Liam Quinn, organised a big surprise party – an American Wake – for me at the Morrissey Whelan Dance Hall before I left. They gave me a nice going-away present: some money to get me started in America.

Then, at the end of April, I went back to the island and to Coumeenole to say my goodbyes to family and friends. We had another American Wake up in my uncle Pats Tom's place on the island that was vacant at the time. I brought over a keg of Guinness for the occasion.

I travelled to America on a steamship, the RMS *Queen Mary*, from Southampton in England. You could go over by airplane by

Mike Carney sailed aboard the RMS *Queen Mary*, shown here arriving in New York in July 1947 on its maiden post-war voyage.

then, but that was far too expensive for me. I took a ferry from Blackrock in Dublin to Holyhead in England. Mary Ward came to the ferry terminal to see me off. As I was departing, I said to her, 'I hope I'll see you again.' She said, 'Well, we'll see.' There were no commitments. As a going-away present, Mary gave me a fine Sheaffer's pen and pencil set. It was gold and engraved with my name and the departure date. In the box was a note that said, 'Whether you travel by air or by sea, may you land on the shore of success.' She asked me to write often.

Of course, I got a big goodbye kiss. And we cried too. I told her I might be back again, depending on how it went.

From Holyhead I took a train all the way across the country to Southampton on the south coast. The trip took all night. We boarded the *Queen Mary* the very next morning. She was both big and beautiful. She had been a troop carrier in the war and had since

been completely renovated. I had a stateroom with two bunks. There was a man from Scotland in the other bunk. He snored like hell and kept me up all night.

My ship sailed for America on 5 May 1948. We had a good time on board. Spirits were high with anticipation. There was great '*craic*'. But I was also a little sad too. I used to sit down and talk to myself. And sometimes I cried. I hoped I was doing the right thing. There was a big celebration on the ship the night before we landed in New York. We had more than a couple of drinks.

When we came into New York Harbor on the morning of 10 May 1948, we all went up on the deck to see the sights. There were so many people on the left side of the ship that I thought it would tip over and sink. I looked at the skyscrapers of New York and I thought they must touch the sky. I was amazed at the height of them. Who could have built them? How did they do it?

I saw the Statue of Liberty and I thought she was going to reach right out and shake my hand. I thought she was trying to welcome me to this country. It was like she was saying, 'You'll be well received; you'll be well taken care of.' I was overjoyed.

The famous Ellis Island immigration centre was being phased out at the time. Instead, we had gone through a United States Customs inspection even before we got on the ship back in Southampton. We disembarked at Pier 69 on the Hudson River. It was a very hot day and I wasn't used to that kind of heat and humidity. I was sweating like never before in my life. I did not think I could stand it.

I had to show my immigration papers to an officer in uniform. They were all in order. I came with only one suitcase. There was nothing in it but my clothes – my only worldly possessions. I had less than a hundred dollars in my pocket.

My uncle Tom and his daughter Helen were picking me up. I had never met them before and they had never met me. I wrote to them before I left Ireland, telling them what I would be wearing when I got off the ship, a black pinstriped suit, so they could pick me out of the crowd. Fortunately, they found me in that huge gang of people and gave me a big bear hug. I thought they'd squeeze the life out of me.

Sporting his new suit, Mike Carney (right) stands with his immigration sponsor, his uncle Tom Carney, shortly after arriving from Ireland.

We went straight from the pier to Grand Central Terminal on 42nd Street by taxi. From there, we took a train to Springfield. It took about three and a half hours.

Welcome to Springfield

To tell the truth, I wasn't quite sure what to make of Springfield when I first arrived. It certainly was not as big and lively as Dublin.

In fact, it was pretty quiet by comparison. There was not as much to do, and it certainly did not have the same social life. But the important things were the jobs, and the money, and the possibility of advancement. This was America, the land of opportunity.

I lived with my uncle Tom Carney at 11 Sherbrooke Street. It was a single-family home; a nice tidy place with three bedrooms. I had my own bedroom on the second floor.

Boy, was it ever hot! We didn't have air conditioning in them days. And then there was the cold and snow in the winter. I think it took more than a year to get used to the weather extremes. After my arrival, I bought myself some American clothes – Bermuda shorts! My American family members had a big welcoming party for me at my uncle Tom's house. All my aunts and uncles and cousins came in and they each gave me ten or twenty dollars. I thought it was great. I thought, 'I don't even have to work in this country. Unbelievable!'

That notion didn't last very long. I knew I needed to get a job and settle down. I wanted to be something other than a barman when I came to in America. I wanted better pay and benefits. I was concerned about my legs over time with all the standing on the job, and I didn't like listening to complaints and taking care of situations when customers got out of line and you had to shut them down. I thought I could do better. It was a great time to be looking for a job in America. The job discrimination against the Irish that my father found when he first came to America was gone. Now, America needed workers.

My uncle Tom had three daughters. I called him 'Pop Pop'. He watched out for me. He was my mentor. His daughter Helen was married to a man who worked for the Great Atlantic and Pacific Tea Company, A&P Supermarkets. It was a huge company. Billy Keane was his name and he kept track of the inventory in A&P stores. Billy made arrangements for me to get an interview.

At that time, A&P had twelve stores just in Springfield alone. Their hiring office was downtown on Worthington Street. I was interviewed by a Mr Philip Larkin, an Irishman. Well, fortunately, I got the job. My Irish connection with Larkin certainly did not

hurt. But I had never been in a supermarket before in my life. I didn't know the first thing about them. I was about to learn.

Bringing the Family to America

One of the main reasons I emigrated to America was to help my family out and to give them the opportunity to come to America if they wished to do so. So, after I arrived, I became a kind of emigration coordinator, helping my brothers and sisters to come over to America. This involved finding sponsors for each of them and moving all the necessary paperwork along. A sponsor had to be an American citizen and a homeowner and could bring over no more than three persons. The sponsor was responsible for you for a period of five years until you qualified to become an American citizen. Becoming a citizen was optional, but we all did so. We felt that if we were going to take advantage of the opportunities of America that we should be citizens and participate in the political process.

After me, the next to emigrate was my brother Maurice who was sponsored by our uncle Maurice Carney. He came about six months after I arrived in Springfield. Then came my brother Paddy, also sponsored by my uncle Maurice, and then my sister Maureen, sponsored by my uncle Tom Carney. I paid for Paddy and Maureen to come over and, of course, they eventually paid me back.

Martin was then sponsored by my uncle Maurice. Then my uncle Tom sponsored Billy. Finally, Maurice Fitzgerald, who was married to my aunt on my mother's side, Nance Daly Fitzgerald, sponsored Tom. So after three or four years, there were seven Carneys of my generation living in Springfield.

Maurice went to work at John H. Breck Company, the shampoo factory in West Springfield. Martin worked for H.L. Handy Company, a meatpacker, and eventually as a truck driver with Burke Beverage, a liquor distributor. My sister Maureen got a job with a restaurant.

Doing All Right in America

Three of my brothers, Paddy, Tom and Billy, went to work for the Springfield Gas Light Company. Paddy was even drafted and required to serve in the United States Army during the Korean War, although he did not actually have to fight in Korea. These were steady jobs and our income was enough to support a pretty good lifestyle, much better than we would have had back on the island.

We always said, 'We're doing all right in America!' This was one of our favourite expressions. We made a good living in Springfield. Our lives were much improved. We were living the American dream.

The Name Game

Our family name in Ireland was 'Ó Ceárna'. When we came to America, we all dropped the 'Ó' in our last name. This shortened and 'Americanised' our name. It was common among Irish people. We used to say that we dropped the 'Ó' in the ocean when we came over. My great aunt Nellie, the first in our family to go to America, went by the last name of 'Carney' when she arrived. When my father went to America, he went by 'Carney' during his first stay, but by 'Kearney' the second time. The confusion begins.

When my uncle Tom filled out my immigration affidavit, he spelled my last name 'Carney' with a 'C' just like he spelled his own name. When my brothers and sister came over, their name was spelled with a 'C' too. But later when they became American citizens, all of them except my sister Maureen changed their name to 'Kearney' with a 'K'. Frankly, I didn't understand it. There are only eighteen letters in Irish and the letter 'K' is not one of them. Why would they use a 'K' in their name? I did not want to argue with them. I said, 'I'm going to be an Irishman with a "C"'. I always teased them, accusing them of not even knowing how to spell their own name. Sometimes people would get confused because the brothers had different spellings of our last names. They thought it was odd. It didn't bother me one bit. To each his own!

Mary Ward's Emigration

When I got to America, I wrote to Mary Ward in Dublin and she wrote back to me in Springfield. I told her about what I was doing, and the money I was making, and the company I was working for. It enticed her. Which, of course, is exactly what I was trying to do.

I told Mary that, if she wanted to come to America, my uncle Tom would prepare the necessary affidavit for her. Eventually, in 1949, she decided to emigrate to Springfield. She paid her own way over. She told her friends in Dublin that if she didn't like it, she would be back. She was promised her job back at Powers Hotel if things did not work out for her in America.

Mary went back home to Frenchpark for a few days to say goodbye to her mother before going to America. (Her father had died when she was young.) Coincidently, while she was at home, she attended the funeral of Douglas Hyde, the founder of the Gaelic League and the first President of Ireland.

Mary sailed for America on the SS *America* from Cork. It took six days to cross the Atlantic. She arrived in New York on 12 August 1949, at the same pier where I had arrived the year before. It was yet another hot day.

Mary travelled with my sister Maureen and one of my sister's friends from West Kerry, Ilene Malone who settled in the state of Rhode Island. My brother Maurice and I picked them up at the pier. I had been in America for over a year and Maurice for six months. So we had become 'Americanised'. We knew the lie of the land.

We took a taxi from the pier to the fancy Hotel Commodore on 42nd Street where we had lunch before taking the train to Springfield from Grand Central Terminal.

Our taxi was going down a busy New York street like a bat out of hell. Mary had never moved so fast in her whole life. She was terrified. A city construction gang was repairing the street at the time. There was an open manhole with a pile of bricks next to it. Well, the taxi knocked one of the bricks down into the manhole. Suddenly, a huge man came up out of the manhole, and he was

mad as a hornet. The brick must have conked him on the head. He was yelling and screaming at the top of his lungs. But the taxi driver just took off speeding down the street. We were all laughing to beat the band. To us, it was quite comical.

Mary stayed with my uncle Tom for a few days, and then she moved to her own room in my friend John McDonald's house on Judson Street, near Liberty School. McDonald was from Ventry.

Mary did housekeeping in the wealthy Springfield suburb of Longmeadow for a little while. Then she got a job at the A&P warehouse on Liberty Street, packing bacon for sale in grocery stores. A lot of Irish girls worked there. I got her the job and it worked out well for her.

Marriage

Around Christmas in 1949 I asked Mary to marry me. It was about four months after she arrived in Springfield. Two friends of mine drove me up to Holyoke, just north of Springfield, to a jewellery store to buy a diamond engagement ring. I had heard about an Irish jeweller there who would give me a fair deal. I didn't own a car at the time. I told my friends they would have to bring me up to Holyoke again to return the ring to the store if Mary turned me down.

I really did not know for sure what Mary would say and was very nervous on the night I proposed. We were out together having a few drinks. I needed to get up some courage.

Well, at the end of the night, I popped the question. And she said, 'yes.' No hesitation. What a relief! And a return trip to the jeweller up in Holyoke wasn't necessary.

There was a stag party for me at a place called Ireland 32 (named for the thirty-two counties in Ireland) in downtown Springfield thrown by my Gaelic footballer friends and a shower for Mary thrown by the ladies at the Marconi Club on Hungry Hill. They were basically fund-raisers to help pay for our honeymoon.

We were married in Our Lady of Hope Church in Springfield on 30 September 1950. Father John J. Power, the pastor, said

Mr and Mrs Michael Joseph Carney pose for a wedding portrait.

the Mass. My brother Maurice was the best man and my sister Maureen was the maid of honour. Mary didn't have any relatives in Springfield and she had, of course, been friendly with my sister Maureen for a couple of years.

We had a big wedding reception in downtown Springfield at Ireland 32 and had a live band and a catered meal. Even Father Power came.

Then we went on a honeymoon for a whole week in New York City. We stayed at the Taft Hotel, a tall building with a big beautiful

The new Mr and Mrs Mike Carney enjoy a drink at the bar at the top of the Empire State Building in New York.

lobby with very nice finishes and fine guest rooms. It was rated as one of the best hotels in New York. We toured all the sights. We went up to the observation deck on top of the Empire State Building, the tallest building in the world at the time. The view was even better than the view from the Crow back on the island.

We went to a restaurant near our hotel called The Black Forest. It was the nicest restaurant that we'd ever been to. It was quite fashionable at the time with great food; it was very expensive. We also went to Jack Dempsey's, the restaurant owned by the famous champion boxer. He had lots of pictures of his fights on the walls. We were thrilled.

And I played a game of Gaelic football in New York's Gaelic Park, a playing field up in the Bronx, a borough of New York City. Mary and I had gone to see a game and word spread that a Gaelic footballer from Ireland was in the stands. So they invited me to play. They gave me a uniform and paid me $25 for my effort. Yes, it certainly was a week to remember.

When we got married, we had about $300 to our name. This was actually a pretty big sum of money at the time.

After the honeymoon, we lived at the corner of Liberty and Carew streets in Springfield on the third floor of an apartment building. Was it ever hot! Our apartment was up under the flat roof of the building where the hot sun beat down all day and there was no air conditioning to give us some relief. We quickly moved to 117 Mooreland Street. It was a bigger and nicer first-floor apartment in a two-family house, right next to my aunt Brigit who was married to my uncle Maurice. Yes, my aunt on my mother's side got married to my uncle on my father's side – they were no relation.

We got our first television set when we lived on Mooreland Street. The first programme we watched was the Saturday night fights. One of the boxers was named Moses Ward. I teased Mary, saying that he must be a cousin of hers from back in Roscommon. But Moses turned out to be a big black guy. And boy, could he fight. He was a true champion!

American Citizenship

I became an American citizen on 15 January 1954. Judge Edward McCauley administered the oath of citizenship in Superior Court in Springfield. There were thirteen or fourteen of us being sworn in that day, including my brother Paddy. The judge gave a brief speech. He said that he wanted us to become citizens, but he wanted us to maintain our ethnic heritage. I liked that a lot. It was the same as my own view on the subject.

Mike Carney's Certificate of Naturalisation as an American citizen, dated 15 January 1954.

I proudly took the oath of citizenship in a loud, clear voice, with an Irish accent, of course. I obviously love Ireland. But I love America too. I don't see a contradiction. After all, everybody loves both parents.

We left the courthouse and went up to American Legion Post 430 on Liberty Street in the Hungry Hill neighbourhood to celebrate the special occasion. We had more than a few drinks that night.

Mary got her citizenship a year later because she emigrated a year later than I did. She became a citizen on 3 June 1955. When she did, she changed her name to 'Maureen.' We talked about it and we decided that 'Maureen' sounded more Irish than 'Mary'. So 'Maureen' it was.

Our Lady of Hope Church, Hungry Hill, Springfield.

Hungry Hill

When I came over to America, my family all lived in the Hungry Hill neighbourhood in Springfield. It was on the top of a hill, about a mile up from Main Street. There are a couple of theories on how Hungry Hill got its name. Some think that it's a tribute to Hungry

Hill on the Beara Peninsula near Cork. Some think it's a mocking reference to the huge quantities of food that people bought for their growing families. Still others think that a popular policeman gave the neighbourhood its name in the early 1900s. The legend is that he was frustrated at the lack of restaurants in the area where he could get a bite to eat while on patrol and he gave it the nickname 'Hungry Hill.' But whatever the source of the name, there wasn't really any hunger in the neighbourhood. It was the opposite of the conditions during the Famine back in Ireland.

Lots of Irish people lived in Hungry Hill, along with some Italian, Greek and Jewish people. In fact, it was mostly Irish at one time, back in the 1950s and 1960s. They were good working-class people. Everybody knew everybody.

Hungry Hill was a nice clean place to live. It had tree-lined streets and mostly two-family homes with porches at the front and neat lawns. There were stores on the main streets. Everything was tidy and well kept.

The heart of the neighbourhood was Our Lady of Hope parish. It was a nearly all-Irish congregation. Some people would even speak Irish outside the church on a Sunday morning after Mass. Families would send their kids to Our Lady of Hope School. The Irish always pushed education.

Hungry Hill reminded me of the island. People were always helping one another. People would help other people to get jobs and babysit for each other. It was close-knit. If there was an accident, a hospitalisation, an operation, or if somebody died, they would run a benefit event where people would socialise to raise money for the family. Irish social events were usually held in downtown Springfield. There was Ireland 32 and Tara Hall and the John Boyle O'Reilly Club.

We played lots of cards in the neighbourhood, including high-low-jack, just like back on the island. Maureen and I would go to our friends, the Longs, to play cards. I remember we all had hula-hoops one night when they were popular. It was wild.

We always stayed current on the news from Ireland. We got letters from West Kerry and we would share the news, just like

back on the island. And we would write letters back home to let our relatives know how we were doing in America. I would send money back to my family when I could.

My friend Maurice Brick, who emigrated from West Kerry and who lives in New Rochelle, New York, would send me his copy of *The Kerryman* every week. I would read it and then we would circulate it all around Hungry Hill. It was certainly a well-read newspaper! I suppose we were too cheap to buy our own subscription. I still read *The Kerryman* every single week. Maurice has been sending it to me for over twenty-five years.

St Patrick's Day was always a major event on Hungry Hill. Every year we would hang a large banner across Carew Street near Our Lady of Hope Church. It said 'Hungry Hill – Home of the Irish'. A whole gang of us marched in the big St Patrick's Day Parade up in Holyoke. It is the second-largest St Patrick's Day Parade in America after Savannah, Georgia. Lots of Irish went up to Holyoke with our kids to participate in the festivities.

There were plenty of package stores and bars on Hungry Hill where you could get some strong drink. Nobody ever died from thirst. On Sunday, package stores were closed but you could get liquor from a drug store if you had a prescription from a doctor. We used to joke, 'Did you get your prescription today?'

I suppose that there was plenty of drinking going on among the Irish in Springfield. But I always felt that the Irish didn't drink any more than people of any other nationality. Unfortunately, there were many families in Springfield that suffered from an alcoholic family member. And the Irish certainly had their share of this curse, the Carney or Kearney family included. I was never a big drinker. I was always too busy.

My generation was very hard working. A lot of guys worked a couple of jobs. We made sure our children got a good education and good jobs. The next generation was better educated than we were. They got even better jobs. They were making even more money. When they started their own families, our kids tended to move to the suburbs around Springfield, like Wilbraham, Longmeadow,

East Longmeadow, West Springfield and so on. They wanted a quieter area and a bigger backyard. And they wanted to live in single-family homes. I suppose it was just like the young people of my generation leaving the island for a better way of living.

Today, Hungry Hill is not an Irish neighbourhood. Other nationalities moved in from other places, especially Puerto Rico, in the 1980s, the 1990s and after the turn of the millennium. There are Hispanics and African Americans and lots of others. You don't hear Irish on Hungry Hill any more; you hear Spanish instead.

The neighbourhood has deteriorated a bit. The houses are not as well kept. Our Lady of Hope School has closed. And even our beloved Our Lady of Hope Church closed in 2011, after two parishes were combined. It is sad to watch the passing of these Irish institutions. Today, the only Irish centre in Springfield is the John Boyle O'Reilly Club.

Irish-American Politics

Politics was always a big thing in Springfield, especially on Hungry Hill. There were elections for City Council and State Representative and Mayor and the United States Congress. Naturally, most of the winners were Irish. Eddie (Edward P.) Boland from Mooreland Street was elected to Congress. Dan (Daniel M.) Brunton, Tommy (Thomas J.) O'Connor, Billy (William C.) Sullivan and Mary Hurley were elected Mayor. Hurley was the first woman mayor of Springfield and is now a judge. 'Red' (James) Bowler, Arthur McKenna and our own relative, Sean Cahillane, served as State Representatives in Boston. Mike (Michael J.) Ashe serves as Sheriff of Hampden County and has served in this capacity for almost forty years. Mike is married to my niece Barbara, another Carney and a Blasket descendant.

Later, we elected Richie (Richard E.) Neal as Mayor of Springfield and then to Congress when Eddie Boland retired in 1987. Richie was from down the hill, in Sacred Heart parish, but he is certainly one of us – a true Irishman.

Congressman Neal has been highly involved in the Irish peace process and a devoted supporter of our efforts to preserve the memory of the island over the years. We are very proud of him.

Blasket Islanders in Hungry Hill

The islanders in my generation that came to the Springfield area were just following earlier emigrants to Springfield who then sponsored the new come-overs. I really don't know why the first emigrants chose Springfield. There is a story that it was a man named Guiheen and that he came to Springfield before the Civil War in America, maybe in the 1850s, but I have no way of knowing. In any event, somebody from the island must have come over first, and then others followed. Hartford was the same way. There were quite a number of former islanders living in Hungry Hill, about two dozen. They included:

- From my father's generation: his brothers, Tom, Mike and Maurice Carney, their sister Neilí Carney Sullivan, Neilí's husband, Tom Sullivan, and two unrelated islanders, Patrick 'Cogant' Connor and Catherine 'Fillie' Carney Garvey.
- From my generation: yours truly and my siblings Maurice, Martin, Paddy, Thomas and Billy, and Maureen Carney Oski; our first cousins Eileen Kearney Cahillane, Mairéad Kearney Shea, Sister Mary Clemens, SP (Mary Kearney), Catherine Kearney Moore and Thomas Kearney; and other unrelated islanders, Thomas and Maurice Kearney, Eilís O'Connor Sullivan, Thomas Crohan, son of Tomás Ó Criomhthain, the original islandman himself, and Mike Guiheen.

I am sure that there were other islanders, but I just can't remember them all. It was as if a chunk of the island community had been uprooted and relocated to Hungry Hill. Since Hungry Hill was mostly Irish, the islanders fitted in quite well. But they were still minor celebrities because of all the folklore about the island. It was not uncommon for them to be referred to as 'the islanders'. And, of course, we all took great pride in being from the island.

US Congressman Richard E. Neal, Democrat, from Springfield, Massachusetts, who has family roots in Ventry, has been an effective advocate for the preservation of The Great Blasket Island.

Other islanders settled in Hartford, Connecticut, just 25 miles south of Springfield. They included the Keanes, with four sisters, the O'Connors, the Guiheens, and still another family of Kearneys, no relation.

My cousin, Eileen Kearney from the island, got married to Maurice Cahillane from Comeen, Ballydavid. Eileen left the island at sixteen and lived with me for a time in Dublin before coming to America.

Maurice was nicknamed 'The Prince' of Hungry Hill. He was a big personality, like Kruger himself. He would stand out and tell you about anything and everything with lots of confidence. Everybody on Hungry Hill knew 'The Prince'. Unfortunately, his back got hurt on the job up at Monsanto Chemical Company in the Indian Orchard section of Springfield and he was disabled for many years. But it did not diminish his big personality one bit.

Eileen and The Prince had five children, who were about the same age as my own. Their son Sean is a politician, a former state representative and public official. He has been a great leader in support of the preservation of the island over a very long period of time.

Nearly all the children of island families achieved success in this country. There were many more opportunities than back on the island and they made the most of it. They became teachers, policemen, nurses, politicians, government officials, bankers, businessmen and businesswomen. It was a source of great pride in the community.

My Career

I worked for A&P supermarkets for over twenty-seven years. My first assignment was grinding Eight O'Clock Coffee, Bokar Coffee and Red Circle Coffee in the A&P in Indian Orchard, a section of Springfield. The coffee beans came in a big 100 lb burlap bag. I ground it up in a machine and packaged it in 1 lb bags, ready for sale to the customers.

I went from there to the dairy department and then to other areas of the store and then to other stores. There was always an incentive to advance. I became assistant manager in the South End store on Main Street in Springfield and later assistant manager in the bigger State Street store.

I bought my first car when I was working at the A&P. Before then, I used to have to take the bus everywhere, even to work. I paid just a $100 for a used Hudson. It was a beauty. I didn't even have a driver's licence when I bought it. It was green, for the Irish. Every single car I have owned since has been green. And, of course, green was the Carney family colour for our sheep on the island. I applied for a licence plate that read 'BLASKET'. But I got 'BLASKT' instead because there was a limit of six letters on the plate. Because my licence plate was so unusual, I couldn't hide anywhere in Springfield.

A&P eventually sent me to school in Boston for management training for a week. They were a very big company with more than 15,000 stores in America. I also took a course in business administration at the High School of Commerce two nights a week. It was a good course and it helped me in advancing my career.

Eventually, I got my own managership and worked for five years as an A&P manager. I was even applying the management training I got in the bar business back in Dublin. At one point, I managed the store on Liberty Street in Springfield right in my home neighbourhood of Hungry Hill. Sure enough, the store's sales went up. Everybody in Hungry Hill came in to see Mike Carney. A&P was pretty happy with me. I was making good money for them! Then they sent me back to State Street as manager. That store was tough. It was in the 1960s, and the neighbourhood had started to deteriorate. You had to keep your eye on shoplifting. I had a reputation as a good man for dealing with shoplifting. But eventually I got tired of it, so I requested a transfer and they sent me to the big new store in Enfield, Connecticut.

Over the next couple of years, I worked in stores in Hartford, West Hartford, Wethersfield, Hazardville, and Willimantic, all south of Springfield in Connecticut. This involved a long drive to and from work every day. A&P was using me as a kind of a troubleshooter. I was always going to a store where they had just fired the manager and I would hold the fort for a while, straightening out problems until they hired a new manager. Then I was sent on to a new store. Those last five years with the A&P were

Mike Carney worked at this A&P Supermarket on Main Street in Springfield's
South End neighbourhood. Note the snow on the sidewalk.

not easy. It was one tough situation after another. I was ready to
move on to something else.

In 1975, a new Hampden County Hall of Justice was being
built in downtown Springfield. I went to see Steve Moynahan, a
lawyer and Hampden County Commissioner, about a job in the
new building. Steve said, 'I am sorry to tell you, Mike, but you're
not the only one who applied for these jobs.' I remember one night
I closed up the A&P store in Willimantic at midnight, and drove
home on the back roads. It was a long drive, about 40 miles. Too
long a drive . . . I got home about one o'clock in the morning and
was exhausted.

The very next morning, the phone rang. A secretary said, 'Mr
Moynahan wants to talk with you.' He came on the phone and
said, 'Mike, I think we can start you off in the Hall of Justice. There
is an opening for a security officer.' That was great news indeed!
So, I left A&P in 1975 after twenty-seven years with the company.
I retired from the Amalgamated Meat Cutters Union and got a
union pension.

Doing All Right in America

In my new job, I was in charge of security at the main entrance to the courthouse. I operated a metal detector. But I was also a kind of public relations man. The hours were great, 7 a.m. to 3 p.m., just five days a week. In the supermarket, there was no end to the hours. I got to know all the lawyers and the judges. I loved all the humorous give-and-take every day at work.

Tom Begley was my supervisor. He asked me one day if I liked my new job. I told him it was like dying and going to heaven. I was now into public relations where personality was important.

I also found time to 'moonlight', painting houses with my brother Maurice. We called ourselves 'The Island Painters'. Our motto was 'We do a good job cheap'. I'd say we painted twenty-five to thirty houses in the Springfield area over the years. I don't know how we found the time. But the extra money sure came in handy.

Gaelic Football in America

I have always believed that the Irish should keep together and keep our traditions alive in America.

A group of about twenty of us decided to play Gaelic football. We played other teams from Massachusetts and Connecticut. There were teams from Springfield, Hartford, Holyoke, Albany, New Haven and Bridgeport. Our home games were played at Pratt Field at Springfield College. We would charter a bus for the away games and have a social event in the evening. We had up to 3,000 people at some games. We practised in the evenings at Van Horn Park right on Hungry Hill. Mostly, it was good clean fun. But sometimes it was rough.

Hartford always had a tough football team, and I told our team we needed to be even tougher. The Springfield–Hartford game always seemed to end in a fight. When we played in Hartford, we played in Colt Park, adjacent to the Colt Manufacturing Company factory that made the famous pistols. Nobody ever knew who won the game. And then, of course, we'd have some beer at a big get-together for both teams afterwards.

The Springfield Gaelic Football Team poses with Mike Carney, manager, at right.

I played some Gaelic football myself, but I was mostly an organiser. I was secretary-treasurer, manager and later president of the Southern New England Gaelic Football League for three years. Springfield did pretty well in that league. We won three New England championships in five years.

My brother Martin played Gaelic football too. He played his first game in America on the very first day he arrived in Springfield from Ireland. It was held on the old so-called 'cowflop' field off Nottingham Street in Hungry Hill. In fact, Martin met his future bride, Eleanor D'Anjou, at that very game. As they say, the rest is history.

Teaching Irish in Springfield

Of course, Irish was the only language spoken on the island. It is part of the West Kerry Gaeltacht. But there was no need for

emigrants to speak Irish in America. Some of us would speak it just for the fun of it – just to keep the language alive.

I taught Irish at night at Springfield's High School of Commerce, beginning in about 1955 or so. It was sponsored by the Adult Education Department of the Springfield Public Schools. They taught Irish, Spanish, French and Italian – the languages of all the nationalities that were living in Springfield at the time. I applied for the Irish teaching job and, to my delight, I got it. Finally, I was a teacher. I was not exactly the kind of teacher I had in mind when I was a kid growing up on the island, but I had finally made it. I didn't have a college degree, but I was in my glory.

The students were mostly adults; quite a few were members of the Ancient Order of Hibernians, an Irish fraternal organisation. I taught conversational Irish and some writing. We didn't get into the grammar to any great extent because it is rather difficult with the unusual pronunciation, the silent consonant, the long vowel and so on. The main challenge was lack of practise. The students did not have the opportunity to hear people speaking Irish other than in class. Once in a while, I would run into my students at the John Boyle O'Reilly Club and we would speak in Irish with each other. I tried to teach my own children Irish, but they didn't keep it up and they lost it over time. For them, Irish just didn't have much value. They still know a couple of phrases, but not much.

There was no end to my efforts to preserve Irish. We had a small dog named Ginger, a Lhasa Apso. I used to tell her to sit down in Irish (*'suigh síos'*) and, after a while, she did it. Then I'd give her a biscuit and then tell her in Irish to give me her paw (*'tabhair dom do lámh'*) and, after a while, she would do it. She was a very smart dog.

I used to say that I had the only Irish-speaking dog in America. One time, I was interviewed by a reporter for *The Irish Echo*, an Irish-American newspaper. I told them about Ginger and they printed the story about 'the Gaelic-speaking dog' in Springfield, Massachusetts.

The new John Boyle O'Reilly Club on Progress Avenue in Springfield opened in March 1972.

The John Boyle O'Reilly Club

Together with my Gaelic football buddies, I applied for membership in Springfield's John Boyle O'Reilly Club in 1960. The club was founded in 1880 and was named after the Irish patriot and writer who was exiled from Ireland to Australia because of his political activity. He later escaped to America and was eventually the editor of *The Pilot*, the Catholic newspaper in Boston.

When I came to America, I seemed to have more interest in our Irish heritage than some of the other come-overs. To each his own.

I wanted to keep my Irish heritage alive, particularly my connection with the island. The John Boyle O'Reilly Club seemed like just the place to do it. It was at 1653 Main Street in downtown, on the second floor. There were narrow stairs up from Main Street. A lot of guys fell down those stairs, but they never felt a thing . . . The club had fifty members when I joined. Many of the existing members were not very active and the place itself was in bad shape. After just a year, the Gaelic footballers proposed me for president. And, to my surprise, I was elected!

I told the members that we had to fix the place up, and do more business and make more profit. I used to read our financial reports and it would make me shiver. So we painted the place to make it more presentable. We instituted volunteer bartending where everybody took their turn. You could keep your tips. There was some complaining, but it saved the club some money and it worked out well. We brought in bands from New York and from all over Ireland. We organised a Ladies Auxiliary and lots of women got involved. The membership grew. People started to believe.

But I felt that the current location was no place for us. We were paying rent and the building was in bad shape. So we started a building fund to accumulate the money to improve our facilities.

We found the shell of an unfinished new building on Progress Avenue in an industrial park in Springfield. It had no heat or electricity or plumbing. But I liked the site and name of the street – 'Progress Avenue'. We eventually agreed on a price. The purchase was approved by the membership.

But we still needed a mortgage. We applied at about half a dozen banks and were turned down by every one of them. Banks were worried about loans to social clubs. When I was away from work at the banks, I told my second in command that if my boss called to tell him I was at a wake. Eventually, Community Savings Bank up in Holyoke agreed to give us a loan. We closed on the deal on the last day of 1970.

Now we had a building, but it was still only a shell. Then we got the members who were construction tradesmen to work on weekends on a volunteer basis for just over a year to fix the place up. The 'new' John Boyle O'Reilly Club opened in March 1972. It was mobbed. I came home at three o'clock in the morning. My lovely wife said, 'You have an awful smell of booze on you.' I told her that a lot of people wanted to buy me a drink. It was a great night of celebration.

A couple of years later, I proposed that the club sponsor charter trips to Ireland from Bradley Field in Connecticut on Trans World Airlines, or TWA. We added a charge of $25 per ticket that would go to the club. After six years, we had raised $68,000. Now we

Marshal Mike Carney
leads Springfield's
delegation in the
Holyoke St Patrick's
Parade in 1973.

had money to pay for more improvements to the club, such as a
kitchen, new counters, new furniture and so on.

The travellers would bring back all kinds of stuff from Ireland.
Suitcases would be packed with potatoes, dillisk, black pudding,
Cadbury chocolate bars and, of course, genuine Irish whiskey.
None of this forbidden cargo was ever disclosed to the customs
people, but nobody ever got caught.

When the club moved to Progress Avenue, I proposed that
it sponsor its own radio programme on WMAS. It was a way to
broadcast Irish news and music and to advertise special events at
the club.

I approached my friend Jimmy Sullivan one Sunday morning
after church and asked him if he would be the show's host. He said

he'd be quite pleased to do so and that his wife, my cousin Peggy, would help out too. A year later, the programme moved to WACE.

The radio programme has now been on the air for forty years. People all over the area listen. I still tune in every Saturday morning for a couple of hours.

One time we took an Irish band from the club on WWLP's *Western Massachusetts Highlights* television show, on St Patrick's Day. Everybody on Hungry Hill watched. There was a dinner afterward at the television station. We were shocked that they served Chinese food on St Patrick's Day! We couldn't believe it.

The club was a big supporter of the St Patrick's Day Parade up in Holyoke. We always sent a big contingent to march down the parade route. I marched so many times, I can't even remember. I was honoured to serve as the Springfield parade marshal in 1973.

The club is one of the few social clubs that is organised as a non-profit corporation. I had to go to a meeting at the Statehouse in Boston to explain our charitable purpose to qualify. We said that we awarded scholarships and sponsored Irish dancing festivals, *feiseanna*, and other cultural events.

The members asked, 'How did you do it?' I told them that I had spoken only in Irish; maybe they didn't understand a word I said.

In 1985, we paid off the club's mortgage early and celebrated with a mortgage-burning celebration.

Over the years, the club's membership kept growing. Today, it is almost up to 1,000 members. It is one of the most active Irish social clubs in America. I retired from the leadership of the club in 1986 after serving twenty-four years in office, sixteen as president and another eight as a member of the Board of Directors. I had a great run. And the club is in great shape today.

The Carney Family in America

Around 1956, Maureen and I bought a two-family house at 550 Armory Street near Our Lady of Hope Church. We lived on the second floor and rented out the first floor. This gave us income to help with the mortgage payments.

We also had a couple of rooms up in the attic. There wasn't a second exit off the third floor, so it was illegal to rent it. Well, our tenants up there were only the come-overs from Ireland who stayed with us temporarily while they got settled. And they played Gaelic football with us too. So we tried our best to keep the illegal apartment quiet. Unfortunately, there was lots of noise and singing – Maureen thought that she'd go out of her mind with the singing and the dancing until all hours of the morning. One time, those guys took two six-packs of beer I had in my refrigerator. They drank all the beer and filled up the empty bottles with water, put the caps back on and put them back in my refrigerator. I blew my stack when I discovered their prank.

The footballers would pay Maureen to wash their football uniforms. In the autumn, when the weather turned colder, she would hang them outside to dry and they would be frozen solid with frost the next morning. One time, the neighbours wanted to know how many people were staying at the house. We told them nothing.

We moved to 174 Middle Street in Hungry Hill in 1965. It was a four-bedroom single-family home. It was time to get away from the ruckus.

Maureen and I had four children: Kathleen, Maureen, Noreen and Michael. We tried to keep up the Irish traditions in our house. They all went to Our Lady of Hope School. And, of course, we spent a lot of time at the John Boyle O'Reilly Club. The girls took up Irish dancing at the club, naturally. Maureen entered step-dancing competitions. She even made an appearance on television.

We had a lot of family fun. It was a lively house. We were involved in all kinds of activities in Hungry Hill. 'Ma Carney', as I called Maureen, kept it all together. It wasn't easy for her. She always kept herself busy around the house and elsewhere and she earned the nickname 'the Roscommon hare'. She was a very special woman.

One of our favourite times of year was our summer vacation at Point-o-Woods on the Connecticut shore of the Atlantic Ocean. The cottage we rented was always full of family and friends. I remember one night we had sixteen people staying with us, all Irish.

For thirty-seven years the Carney family made its home in this four-bedroomed house on Middle Street in Springfield.

The kids went to local high schools and then on to college and into good jobs. Kathleen works in insurance and real estate, Maureen in urban redevelopment, Noreen in facilities management and Mike is a Springfield police detective. I have five grandchildren.

The grandchildren are pursuing their college degrees and are already beginning their own careers.

I am very proud of them all. They have done a lot to better themselves. It is the Irish way. Each generation tries to do better than the one before. And in America, there no limits on what you can accomplish.

I often think about how different our lives and the lives of our children would have been if we still lived back on the island or in back in Ireland. Every time I do, I realise that my decision to emigrate to America was the right one for us. The opportunities in America made all the difference for me, Maureen and our family. I am very grateful for my new life in a new land.

The Carney Family in Ireland

After they left the island, my sister Cáit and her husband, Pádraig 'Sheáisí' or 'Paddy' Ó Cearna, lived in Muiríoch, Ballydavid.

Paddy was a great singer and loved to entertain. He worked in public works for the Kerry County Council and did some fishing too. They raised their own family of three boys and two girls. All their children got a good education. They stayed in the West Kerry area for the most part.

Seán is in the construction business. Paíd works at Louis Mulcahy Pottery. Anthony works for Ballyhea Fisheries. Maureen Moriarty and her husband John own Lord Baker's, a fine restaurant in Dingle. And Eilín Ní Chearna works for Raidió na Gaeltachta.

I went back to Ireland to visit for the first time since my emigration in 1961 on a tour organised by the John Boyle O'Reilly Club. It was fourteen years after I came to America. It was a joyous but tearful reunion with my father and Cáit. We had lots of catching-up to do. I stayed with them in Cáit's house in Muiríoch. It was almost like the old days back on the island.

My father, of course, wanted to know about the people and places he remembered from his time in Springfield. It was great to give him the news from America. He had a wonderful time reminiscing.

On one of my trips back, my father told me an old Springfield story about his brother Mike. There was a man from the island who had come over to Springfield. He was a fella who never took care of himself. He was always chewing tobacco and spitting it out. He'd like to take some drink and get rambunctious.

Somebody told my uncle Mike that this islander had got in some kind of trouble and was left handcuffed to a tree by a police officer who had to leave to answer another call. The police van was on its way to pick him up and take him off to the police station. So my father and my uncle ran over there right away and cut the handcuffs off. Then all three of them hightailed it out of there before the paddy wagon showed up. My father loved to tell that story.

On one of our trips back with the John Boyle O'Reilly Club, my wife Maureen and I visited the abandoned family home back on the island. Only the four outside walls were left. To my surprise, the old cast iron pot oven that my mother used to cook cakes and

The Carney clan in America gathered to celebrate the fiftieth wedding anniversary
of Mike and Maureen Carney (fourth and sixth from the left respectively).

other dishes was sitting right there in what was left of the fireplace.
I couldn't resist. We took it back to Springfield as a memento of my
boyhood home on the island.

Trips back to Ireland involved lots of adventure. One time, my
son Mike went back to West Kerry with my brother Paddy and
John 'Diamond' Shea. On their last night in Dingle, they had quite
a time of it. Bright and early the next morning, they piled into their
rental car and headed for Shannon Airport. My son was driving.
Unfortunately, he swerved to avoid a dog, or at least that was his
story. He rolled the car over on its roof and into a ditch. They were
lucky that nobody was seriously hurt, but they had to take a taxi
on a mad dash the rest of the way to the airport. Later, Mike said
to Paddy on the plane, 'I can't believe we're alive after that episode.'
Paddy just said it was the luck of the Irish.

My Father's Death

My father died of old age in Dingle Hospital on 1 February, St
Bridget's Day, in 1968. He was almost eighty-six. Six of his children

Cáit Uí Chearna at her knitting.

from America went back to Kerry for his funeral. We got a barrel of Guinness and some whiskey. We gave the poor man a fine send-off in high style.

His body was brought to the church in Dunquin where it stayed overnight. There was a Mass and he was buried the following day. Since the old cemetery next to the church was full by then, he could not be buried with my mother. Instead, he was buried in the new

Four of Cáit's children gather with Mike Carney at the Blasket Centre in 2012. Standing (*l–r*) are Maureen Moriarty, Paíd Ó Cearna, Eilín Ní Chearna, and Seán Ó Cearna.

cemetery in Dunquin, overlooking the ocean and the island. We went to Kruger's for a couple of drinks afterwards. It was a sombre affair.

My father was quite a man and he had quite a life –a hard life. He was a man of steel, a real islander. He was my inspiration.

Cáit visited us in Springfield a couple of times after my father died, in 1973 and 1989. She would stay for a few days with each one of her siblings. But Cáit did not like America. She found the weather too hot and said that the food disagreed with her stomach. Cáit thought she couldn't adapt to life in America and so was anxious to go back to Ireland. We had a big party for her one night at the John Boyle O'Reilly Club. The place was packed with family and friends.

Cáit's husband Pádraig died in July 1986 at the age of seventy, leaving Cáit alone with their family. My brother Paddy decided to

Mike Carney visits his father's grave in Dunquin.

move back to Ireland after he retired from Baystate Gas Company in 1985. He moved in with Cáit in Muiríoch. But not for long. The damp weather aggravated Paddy's arthritis, so he moved back to Springfield after only about nine months.

Cáit, the poor woman, had a tough life. She did a great job of raising her brothers and her sister under very difficult circumstances. She had a wonderful family of her own. And she took care of my father in his old age. She died, the poor woman, in 2005. I visited her in Muiríoch for the last time in 2001. She was obviously in decline. It was a sad reunion. I think we both knew that it was the last time we would see each other.

I will never forget Cáit for what she did for me and my brothers and sisters. I owe her more than I can ever tell.

Cáit Uí Chearna sits with her dog Spot, a retriever, at her home in Muiríoch in 2001.

Retirement

My wife Maureen retired as a nurse's aide at Springfield's Mercy Hospital in 1985 after twenty years of service. After that, she was a full-time babysitter for two of our grandchildren, Mike and Andrew Hayes, for a number of years. The grandchildren still call me 'Pop-Pop'.

I retired from the Hall of Justice on 16 February 1991, after eighteen years of service. Mayor Mary Hurley proclaimed that day as 'Michael J. Carney Day' in Springfield.

When I look back at my career, I'm proud of what I accomplished. As we used to say all the time, 'We're doing all right in America!' Yes, we did just fine in America.

For me, Cahersiveen was better than the island; Dublin was better than Cahersiveen; and America was better than Dublin. I moved up the ladder.

Cahersiveen and Dublin opened my eyes. People would say, 'Mike, it was a great day for you when you left the island.' Frankly, I could not have endured the aggravation of the island – the weather and the way of living.

Over the years since retirement, we have taken lots of trips with our good friends Mackie (who was from Ventry) and Sheila Garvey. We went to Nova Scotia and Prince Edward Island, both in Canada; to Bermuda, Aruba, and on a Caribbean cruise. We spent the month of March in beautiful, warm Marco Island, Florida, for some twenty-odd years.

When we were in Prince Edward Island, we travelled across the longest bridge in the world, about 9 miles long. I thought to myself that they should build that kind of bridge over to the island from Dunquin.

It is a typical American retirement. It's a big difference from the island where there was really no such thing as retirement. You just helped out with the work of the day as best you could until you couldn't do so any more.

After thirty-seven years on Middle Street, we moved to a condominium in Springfield, called Georgetown, in 2002. At our age, we were having a hard time keeping up with all the maintenance that was involved and we didn't need a four-bedroom house any more. It was tough to leave Hungry Hill, but the old neighbourhood had changed. It was no longer an Irish community.

I have been back to Ireland about twenty-five times over the years. Recently, we have been going back every year for the Blasket Commemoration weekend in late September. I always look forward to my annual visit with great anticipation.

I still keep up with the news from Ireland every week with *The Kerryman*. I always read *The Irish Voice*, *The Irish Echo* and *Ireland of the Welcomes*. And I am still involved in Irish affairs in the Springfield area.

In 2007, I had back surgery for spinal stenosis. The results were highly satisfactory, but we decided to move to Keystone Woods, a new independent-living facility, to get more day-to-day support. It

Mike Carney on his retirement day at the Hampden County Hall of Justice.

worked out very well. My brother Maurice's wife, Joan, lived next door to us.

Unfortunately, the love of my life, Maureen Ward Carney or 'Ma Carney', as I always called her, died of cancer in July 2010 at the age of ninety. She was graceful right until the very end.

Mike and Maureen Carney in 2009 with The Great Blasket Island in the background.

We had a grand send-off for her at Sacred Heart Church, the largest church in Western Massachusetts. There was a lone bagpiper who played the hymn 'Amazing Grace'. It reminded me of the lamenting music back on the island. Of course, we had a reception afterwards at the John Boyle O'Reilly Club.

Maureen and I would have celebrated sixty years of marriage the following September. We had a terrific life together. She put up with a lot as yours truly spent a lot of time on Irish activities. Our life together was quite an adventure in many ways. I miss her dearly every single day. It took me a good six months to get over her passing. But time helps to heal your wounds. Eventually I was able to move on.

I moved again to Bluebird Estates in East Longmeadow in 2010. Yes, I finally made my move to the suburbs. I still give talks on the island and on Ireland. I even teach a little Irish now and again. There's just no rest for an islander.

I listen to Raidió na Gaeltachta faithfully almost all day every day. I get it live right in my apartment on internet radio. There is a five-hour time difference, but that doesn't bother me a bit. It is great to keep up on the news from Kerry and hear the Irish language in news and music.

I still follow the Kerry sports teams back in Ireland and keep in touch with my West Kerry friends who are huge fans. But I am also fan of all the Boston area sports teams, including the Red Sox, the Patriots, the Bruins and the Celtics.

Despite my love for Ireland and the island, I was never tempted to move back after I was established here in America almost sixty-six years ago. I set down new roots in Springfield. I am now a true Irish-American. But now, more than ever, I appreciate my island heritage and I am determined to preserve its legacy.

9. An Island Legacy

Even at the age of almost ninety-three and counting, I am still working to preserve the legacy of my beloved island. I firmly believe that The Great Blasket has earned a special place in Irish history and in the story of the emigration of the Irish people to the United States.

Fortunately, I am not alone. A whole group of people from West Kerry and America have worked tirelessly to perpetuate the traditions and memory of the island.

Edna Uí Chinnéide of Moorestown and her sons, Micheál and Lorcan, have been leading supporters of the island for the past twenty-five years. Edna was married to my second cousin and best friend in Dublin, Caoimhín Ó Cinnéide. (Caoimhín passed away in 1985.)

Edna is a great organiser, fund-raiser, researcher and editor. She is passionate and persistent. She is highly dedicated to the Blasket cause. Her son Micheál is a very special personal friend. He is named after his islander great-grandfather, Micheál 'Mhuiris' Ó Catháin who drowned in a fishing accident back in Cuas an Bhodaigh, near Moorestown. A group of them were fishing for mackerel one night. They overloaded their *naomhóg* and it tipped over in a cove near the pier. It was a tragedy. Micheál graduated from the National University of Ireland (NUI) Galway and got a master of business administration degree from Harvard University in Massachusetts. He has served the Irish government in a number of important positions. Today, he is a director with the Environmental Protection Agency of Ireland.

Mike Carney at ninety years of age.

When Micheál was studying at Harvard and working at the Irish Consulate in New York City, he stayed in our home on Hungry Hill many, many times. He used to say it was his second home. I would tell him stories about the old days on the island. And, of course, we'd go to the John Boyle O'Reilly Club to have a few beers.

The Blasket Island Foundation

In the early 1970s, an American named Taylor Collings from Alabama started buying plots of land on the island. He was planning to create a resort of some type, a kind of 'Blasket Island Ranch'. Some people said he got the idea from the beautiful scenery

Edna Uí Chinnéide
reviews Blasket material
with Mike Carney
and Gerald Hayes in
Dingle.

that was shown in the film *Ryan's Daughter* that was popular at the time. He had big plans. And preservation of the legacy of island was not high on his agenda.

Quite a few former islanders sold their island holdings to Collings. They saw it as an opportunity to sell property that they thought might be worthless. Eventually, he purchased seventeen of the twenty-five private properties on the island. My sister Cáit sold our own family home to Collings for a very small amount of money, maybe £100 or so. She thought that getting £100 in cash was better than nothing. But Collings lost interest in the project for some reason. Maybe he could not get financing – I don't know.

In May 1985, Micheál Ó Cinnéide saw an advertisement in the *Wall Street Journal* offering the island for sale for $900,000. He was shocked. The ownership of the island had passed from Collings to a company called An Blascaod Mór Teoranta, or The Blasket Island, Limited. The company was run by Peter Callery, a solicitor from Dingle, who had been Collings' lawyer, and his brother Jim. They were interested in selling. This was startling news. All of a sudden, people realised that the legacy of the island might be in jeopardy. I immediately said to Micheál, 'over my dead body.' The news motivated me and others to do something about it.

A group of people with various island connections got together and established the Blasket Island Foundation (*Fondúireacht an Bhlascaoid*), a private non-profit organisation in 1987. Its purpose is to keep the spirit of the island alive and to promote its memory.

The Foundation considered trying to purchase the island, but the asking price had been increased to $1 million and that kind of

money was way out of reach. It seemed that the only way to acquire and preserve the island was to get the government involved. As we knew from past experience, that could (and did) take many years.

The Foundation raised money for a study on the creation of a Blasket Centre as a first step in preserving the island's legacy. The big fund-raiser was a raffle. Tickets were $100 apiece. I sold some tickets at the John Boyle O'Reilly Club in Springfield. Good old-fashioned gambling got the ball rolling on the preservation of the island. Because of the professional study commissioned by the Foundation, the Irish government took a serious interest in the project and eventually funded and built the Blasket Centre (*Ionad an Bhlascaoid*) in Dunquin.

Today, the Foundation promotes the island with its annual magazine, *An Caomhnóir*, with the annual 'Blasket Commemoration' (*Ceiliúradh an Bhlascaoid*) conference and with a scholarship programme for the young people of West Kerry.

After the Blasket Centre opened in 1993, the Foundation then pushed for the acquisition of the island land and the creation of The Great Blasket Island National Historical Park. That is a story in itself.

The Blasket Centre/Ionad an Bhlascaoid

The Blasket Centre is located in Dunquin directly overlooking the island, across Blasket Sound. The purpose of the centre is to educate people about the way of life on the island.

Speaking at the centre's dedication ceremony in 1994, Bertie Ahern, then Minister for Finance and later Taoiseach, said, 'I wish to acknowledge that this centre would never have been achieved without the dedication of the *Fondúireacht an Bhlascaoid* and I would like to take this opportunity to publicly recognise that contribution. The *Fondúireacht* is comprised of a group of exceptional people fully dedicated to the preservation of the island.' This was high praise for those involved and it was richly deserved.

The Blasket Centre in Dunquin overlooks Blasket Sound and the island. A statue of
Tomás Ó Criomhthain stands at the left.

On the central plaza that overlooks the island, there is a fine
statue of Tomás Ó Criomhthain looking out towards the island
with the wind blowing in his face. He is holding his hat down on

Mike Carney reads The Kerryman at home in Springfield. This photo is on display
in 'The Springfield Gallery' at the Blasket Centre.

his head and his coat is blowing in the wind. When I think about
it, I nearly cry.

They even have a picture of yours truly, Mike Carney, on display
in a section dedicated to Springfield's island emigrants. I am sitting
on the front stoop of my house on Middle Street in my Bermuda
shorts and bare feet reading *The Kerryman*.

The best indication of the centre's success is the fact that over
40,000 people visit every year. It is one of the biggest tourist draws

in Ireland. The director of the centre is Micheál de Mórdha from Dunquin. He has done a fantastic job of promoting the island over the years. He is constantly researching the history of the island and is extremely knowledgeable about island life. And his son Dáithí is following in his footsteps.

In 2012, Micheál published a book on the social history of the island entitled *Scéal agus Dán Oileáin*, or *The Story and Fate of an Island*. I call Micheál on the telephone just about every week so that I can keep up to date in matters involving the island.

The Great Blasket Island National Historical Park

The island has been pretty much abandoned for sixty years now. The Blasket Centre is a great place for explaining the island's past, but I would like to see the island itself protected for future generations. Today, The Great Blasket is quite a tourist attraction. About 15,000 people a year go into the island on motor boats operated by independent boatmen. Depending on the weather, these ferries depart from Dingle or Dunquin. It can be a rough trip! But, with some many people walking all over the old village, the ruins of the homes need to be preserved and explained, and restroom facilities are needed.

In 1989, under the leadership of then Taoiseach Charlie Haughey, the government adopted An Blascaod Mór National Historic Park Act. This act authorised purchasing most of the island from its current owners by compulsory acquisition, or 'eminent domain' as we would say in America. But An Blascaod Mór Teoranta, the major owner, filed a lawsuit objecting to the compulsory acquisition of the land. Unfortunately, the Supreme Court found that the act was unconstitutional. This was a big setback, of course, but the Foundation continued to work with the government to prepare a management plan for the park.

Martin Nolan, the Kerry County Manager at the time, played a very important role in developing the plan. He was calm, cool and collected. He invited all interested parties to come forward and

A group of US Congressmen visit the Blasket Centre in 2009. (*L–r*) Donald Payne, Richard E. Neal, Nydia Velazquez, Luis Gutierrez and Timothy Murphy with Dr Breandán Ó Cíobháin, genealogist, and Micheál de Mórdha, Centre Director.

speak their mind. He held public forums in West Kerry and even in the Springfield area. He was very fair to all involved. I spoke out at the Springfield forum, urging the Irish government to create the park as soon as possible. It would preserve the island and bring it back to life again.

The biggest obstacle to the creation of the park was still the acquisition of the land. Since compulsory acquisition was now out, the government would need to reach an agreement with the owners.

The Minister for Arts, Sports and Tourism, John O'Donoghue, TD for South Kerry, helped to get a government appropriation to fund the acquisitions. This was critical since there would be no deal without fair compensation to the seller. Then, in 2005, the government approached the Callerys about buying their land. The Callerys wanted permits to operate the visitor services on the island. The permits were issued but they were appealed to An Bord Pleanála in Dublin by two people who wanted to keep the status quo.

I got very frustrated with all the delays. I called *The Kerryman* and told them that there was a book written about the island called *Twenty Years a-Growing*. Now, we had been 'twenty years a-waiting' for the national park. I told them that all the delay was like a kick in the backside. I told them I was speaking from my heart. They printed all this in the newspaper.

Our congressman from Springfield, Richie Neal, strongly supported the park. He got in touch with the then Taoiseach, Bertie Ahern, and urged the government to move the plans for the park forward.

Eventually, An Bord Pleanála denied the appeal in October 2008. In my opinion, they got it right.

Then, in February 2009, the government reached agreement with An Blascaod Mór Teoranta to acquire most of the land. Finally, things started to move forward.

In May 2009, Mary McAleese, then President of Ireland, visited the Springfield area. She met with me, my brother Martin and my cousin Mairéad Kearney Shea, the two local surviving islanders. Of course, I brought up the government's support for the park. She told me not to worry. This was a great relief. Her words meant a lot since they came right from the top.

In June 2012, I was honoured to meet another President of Ireland, Michael D. Higgins, on his visit to Boston. Higgins had previously served in the government as Minister for Arts, Culture and the Gaeltacht. In that job, he was involved in the creation of the Blasket Centre in the 1990s. He was accompanied on his visit to Boston by the current Minister, Jimmy Deenihan, a former Gaelic footballer for Kerry. This was yet another opportunity to emphasise the importance of preserving the island, and their response was very positive. This was even more encouraging news.

But, as in the case of the evacuation, we eventually achieved the goal. The land has been acquired. Work on the park has begun and the improvements so far are terrific. Guides are giving tours of the island. It is not yet officially a national park, but that day will come soon.

(*L–r*) Gerald W. Hayes, Minister Jimmy Deenihan, President Michael D. Higgins, Mike Carney, Maureen Carney Hayes and Michael P. Carney enjoy a moment in Boston.

I suppose I am an impatient man or maybe even a stubborn man. The effort to persuade the government to move forward with the park took many, many years. In some ways it reminded me of the years it took to persuade the government to move the remaining islanders off the island. Unfortunately, governments do not move as fast as one would like.

I think the island deserves the recognition. I certainly hope it happens while I am still living.

Dr Michael Joseph Carney

On a September morning in 2009, my son Mike, my daughter Maureen and her husband Jerry Hayes showed up at our apartment at Keystone Woods, having been tipped off on some very important news. Then the phone rang. It was Micheál de Mórdha calling from the Blasket Centre. He said that he had good news for me.

Dr Carney is flanked by Dr Tadgh Ó Dubhsláine (left) and Dr James Walsh, deputy president, NUI Maynooth.

De Mórdha announced that the NUI Maynooth had decided to award me an honorary doctorate in Celtic literature. He said that it was to be conferred later in the month and that I needed to pack my bags for Ireland. This was a huge surprise! I really didn't know what to make of it! I was to be the recipient of the degree as the oldest surviving islander, but it was being awarded in recognition of the literary contributions of all islanders, living and dead.

For just a brief a moment, I had a flashback. I remembered my old friend Kruger marching into the Dáil with the leather satchel that said 'Maurice Kavanagh, MD'. I was about to be a doctor, just like Kruger.

The whole Carney family went back to Ireland for the ceremony. The degree was formally presented at the Blasket Centre by Dr James Walsh, deputy president of the university. Representing the government at the event was the Minister of State for the Office of Public Works, Dr Martin Mansergh. I was flattered, but I was also humbled. I am just a fisherman's son. I gave a brief acceptance

speech in Irish and in English. It was certainly the proudest moment of my life.

My only complaint on the day was that the colour of the academic gown I had to wear for the occasion was red, a Cork colour. I would have preferred green for Kerry!

When I was a youngster growing up in the island, I passed the Preparatory Examination, but was denied admission to college. Now, in my ripe old age, I was awarded an honorary doctorate. It has been quite a journey. I am proud of my own efforts to advance Irish and the history of the island, but I am a poor substitute for the likes of Ó Criomhthain, Ó Súilleabháin and Sayers. They are the real giants of island literature.

The Great Blasket Island Bursary

At ninety-one years of age, I was back at it again. I was worried that, as time goes on, young people in the West Kerry Gaeltacht might be less interested in the island and that the use of Irish might fade. My suggestion was to create a scholarship or bursary. It would be awarded each year to young Irish-speaking people from West Kerry. The funds would be used for the study of some aspect of Irish language or culture. In my mind this was similar to my family donating the land for the school on the island – even today the Carneys push education.

The Great Blasket Island Bursary was established in 2010 in memory of my deceased wife, Maureen Ward Carney. Contributions were solicited from friends of the island both in Ireland and in the United States. The Carney family made an initial contribution to get the bursary going.

I was pleased to participate in ceremonies at the commemoration in September 2011, presenting the first bursary awards to Colm Galvin of Lispole and Aisling Sullivan of Dingle. They both subsequently attended the University of Limerick. I am very pleased that additional contributions have been received and the Bursary is now in a position to continue for many years to come.

Mike Carney congratulates Colm Galvin and Aisling Sullivan, the first recipients of awards from The Great Blasket Island Bursary.

Living Blasket Islanders

In 2012, there were only ten living native islanders, people who actually lived and grew up on The Great Blasket. I am the oldest living islander. The survivors are:

* LIVING IN IRELAND: Maureen Dunleavy Boland (Mairín Ní Dhuinnshléibhe Uí Bheoláin) of Dublin; Niamh Crohan Leahy (Niamh Ní Chriomhthain Uí Laoithe) of Baile an Lochaigh; Gearóid 'Cheáist' Keane (Gearóid 'Cheáist' Ó Catháin) the last person born on the island and now of Cork; Nell Guiheen O'Shea (Eibhlín Ní Ghuithín Uí Shé) of Comeen, Ballydavid; and Noreen Keane (Nóirín Ní Chatháin) and her sister Margaret Keane Costello (Mairéad Ní Chatháin Uí Choisdealbha) both of Ballyferriter; and my sister Cáit's son Seán Ó Cearna of Ballydavid who lived on the island for a couple of years as a boy before moving to Muiríoch with his parents.
* LIVING IN AMERICA: Mike Carney (yours truly); Maureen Carney Oski (my sister); and Mairéad Kearney Shea (my cousin). All live in Springfield.

Five islanders visit the Blasket Centre in 2009. (*L–r*) Niamh Uí Laoithe, Mairín Boland, Maureen Carney Oski, Nell O'Shea and Pádraig Keane.

That's it; only ten of us left. Unfortunately, all the others are now dead. They are certainly not forgotten. I miss them all very much. But time marches on.

A Personal Legacy

At my personal request, the government has installed a plaque on the island in front of the ruins of the schoolhouse. It reads as follows:

The ruins of the Carney home in 2012, showing conservation work by the government.
Cáit slept in a loft at the right gable. The school is to the left.

I gcuimhne ar mhuintir an Oileáin seo go léir
mar ná beidh a leithéidí arís ann

In English, it reads: 'In memory of all the people of this island
because the likes of them will never be again.' This, of course,
borrows from Ó Criomhthain's famous words from the last line of
The Islandman.

I sincerely appreciate all the opportunities I had in America.
As an emigrant from Ireland, it was up to me to make the most
of it. And I did. But a part of me still lives on the island. As the
islanders pass away, I wanted to see something on the island itself
that would perpetuate their memory. The Blasket Centre and The
Great Blasket Island National Historical Park will show visitors
what it meant to be an islander. They are important parts of my
own legacy. I put my heart and soul into preserving the island and

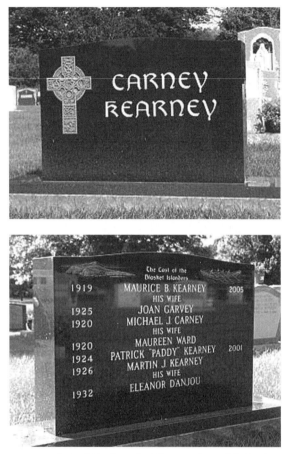

This gravestone in Springfield reflects the different spellings of the family name. In the etching of a *naomhóg* on the right, the four rowers signify the four brothers to be buried at this site.

promoting the advancement of Irish culture in America and back home in Ireland.

I would like to see people of all ethnic backgrounds maintaining their culture, their ideals, the history of their place of birth and, most of all, their heritage. I believe that if you lose your heritage, you might as well lose yourself.

Mike Carney and his son Michael P. Carney visit the island in 2010.

On the granite monument on the Carney family grave in the Gate of Heaven Cemetery in Springfield, we have a drawing of the island and four men rowing a *naomhóg*. The inscription on the gravestone reads, 'The Last of the Blasket Islanders'.

Well, it has certainly been a grand adventure. There have been lots of twists and turns over the years. It has been seventy-five years since I left the island. My love for the island has stayed with me all this time. I have done my best to advance the island. And my family has helped too. It's something in my system. It's in my soul.

So why am I writing these memoirs at the age of almost ninety-three? Tomás Ó Criomhthain once said that he wrote poetry, 'So that I can be living while dead'. That is my reason for writing these memoirs, to keep the memory of the island and the

A restored Blasket home

story of my emigration alive for my descendants and anybody else who might be interested. I can now rest peacefully with my dreams of the island and with the knowledge that the spirit of the island lives on and on through the Blasket Centre, The Great Blasket Island National Historical Park and The Great Blasket Island Bursary.

Now, I can rest easy with the knowledge that the great spirit of The Great Blasket Island will never die. That spirit will live on forever.

The Blasket Sound

The ocean raged and stormed
Crashed upon the rocky shore,
While an old man mourned
His friends and kin the ocean bore.

Waves surged like a beast loosed from its cage.
The desolate islands spoke out to him.
They knew the story of his life and age.
Each wave landed its outlook grim.

Taunting him to come from shore,
Promising all hopes of more,
Death was what the ocean held, nothing more,
Than all dreams of times better than before.

A journey to defeat this beast of impossible power,
To the land of America, the land of opportunity.
Nothing could ever stop the coming of this hour,
A trip of impossible importance to the island community.

From the Blaskets they sailed apart
Leaving behind nothing but wood and stone.
The weight of their memories engulfing their hearts.
They discovered Hungry Hill and called it home.

The stories and legends will live on forever.
His quest had ended, theirs had just begun.
Sometimes the ocean rages still
But for him it always will.

By Devon Bowers, Mike Carney's grandson

Chronology

1882   Seán Tom Carney is born on The Great Blasket Island

1917   Seán Tom Carney marries Nellie Daly (2 March)

1920   Mary Ward born in Frenchpark, Roscommon (23 March)

1920   Mike Carney born on The Great Blasket Island (22 September)

1922   The Irish Free State established (6 December)

1933   Nellie Daly Carney dies (1 July)

1936   Mike Carney completes school on The Great Blasket Island (June)

1937   Mike Carney leaves home for Cahersiveen (January)

1937   Mike Carney leaves Cahersiveen for Dublin (May)

1940   Mike Carney completes apprenticeship at Malloy's pub

1941   The Great Blasket Island school closes

1942   Mike Carney completes junior barman service at Davy Byrnes pub

1943   Mike Carney completes senior barman service at Hennessey's pub

1947   Seán Carney dies (9 January)

1947   Éamon de Valera visits The Great Blasket Island (15 July)

1948   Cáit Uí Chearna moves from The Great Blasket Island to Muiríoch (Easter)

1948   Mike Carney sails for America on *Queen Mary* (5 May)

1948   Seán Tom Carney moves to Muiríoch to live with Cáit Uí Chearna

1949   Mary Ward arrives in America on the SS *America* (12 August)

1950   Mike Carney marries Mary Ward (30 September)

1952   Irish government orders The Great Blasket evacuated (November)

1953	The Great Blasket Island is evacuated (17 November)
1954	Mike Carney becomes an American citizen (15 January)
1955	Mary Ward Carney becomes an American citizen – changes her name to Maureen (3 June)
1972	John Boyle O'Reilly Club moves to Progress Avenue in Springfield
1968	Seán Tom Carney dies in West Kerry
1994	The Blasket Centre opens in Dunquin
2005	Management plan for The Great Blasket Island finalised
2008	The Great Blasket Island planning permits are issued (October)
2009	Blasket land acquired by the Irish government (February)
2010	Guided tours of The Great Blasket Island begin
2010	Maureen Ward Carney dies in Springfield
2010	The Great Blasket Island Bursary established

Acknowledgments

- Mike Carney – for his incredible life story as well as for his precise memory, great patience, good humour, and his monumental dedication to The Great Blasket Island.
- Maureen Ward Carney – for tolerating her islander and his inquisitor as the interviews proceeded over a period of years.
- Maureen Carney Hayes – for seemingly endless editing and for moral support when the process turned daunting.
- Micheál Ó Cinnéide – for editing, fact checking, expert guidance and constant encouragement over the years while the project came together.
- Edna Uí Chinnéide – for her painstaking editing and suggestions to ensure the historical accuracy of the work.
- Micheál de Mórdha – for sharing his wealth of knowledge and for providing access to the full resources of the Blasket Centre/ *Ionad an Bhlascaoid*. His enormous contributions and keen insight provided much-needed depth, particularly focused on the events that led to the evacuation and on land transactions.
- Dáithí de Mórdha – for historical information, particularly on landownership and related matters as well as in reviewing maps, compiling the photographs and in the use of Irish.
- Eilín Ní Chearna – for background information and guidance on the history of the Carney family living in Ireland.
- Pam Robbins – for extraordinary professional editing and contributions to the structure of the tale.
- The Collins Press, who believed that this story is worth sharing and who collaborated with the authors to present it a compelling fashion.

Gerald W. Hayes

Photograph, Document and Quotation Credits

Material incorporated herein is presented courtesy of the following:

National Geographic Traveler: p. 1
Michael P. Carney: p. 2
National Monuments Service and the Blasket Centre: pp. 3 and 184
Michael E. Hayes: 4, 17, 56, 58, 59, 61, 71, 173, 174 and 178
Blasket Centre Archives: pp. 9, 10, 19, 23, 24, 28, 29, 42, 50, 63, 74 (George Thomson),
    75, 91, 94, 107, 120, 124, 125, 128, 187, and 194 (Doncha Ó Conchúir)
Saint Vincent's Church, Ballyferriter: p. 13
Carney family archive: pp. 14, 81, 102, 117, 130, 142, 148, 149, 151, 162, 166, 171
    and 185
National Folklore Collection, University College Dublin: pp. 16 (Carl Von Sydow),
    33, 35, 39 (Teach Mhucrois), 46, 48 (George Chambers), 52 (Carl Von Sydow),
    76 and 89
Board of Trinity College Dublin: pp. 20 (John Millington Synge Collection) and 26
    (Browne Collection)
Thomas H. Mason: pp. 31, 72 and 88
Leslie Matson: p. 57
Oxford University Press: p. 72
Shane Ross: p. 78 and 129
Kim Kane: Kane family archive: p. 84
Gerald W. Hayes: pp. 86, 103, 152, 164, 169, 175, 195 (both) and 196
Houses of the Oireachtas: p. 126
Irish Examiner: p. 137
Cunard Line and Queen Mary Association: p. 140
Office of US Congressman Richard E. Neal: p. 157
Springfield Public Library (Massachusetts): p. 160
Robert Quinn: p. 172
The Republican, Springfield, Massachusetts: p. 177
Roger Hagmann: pp. 181 and 197
Andrew D. Hayes: p. 182
Office of the President of Ireland: p. 189
An Caomhnóir, Fondúireacht an Bhlascaoid: pp. 190, 192, and 193
Devon Bowers: p. 198

Every effort has been made to secure permission from the copyright holders for the use of photographs and other material presented in this book. We apologise for and regret any error or oversight. Please advise the publisher of any corrections that should be made in future editions of this book.

Bibliography

The Blasket Centre Archives (Dunquin, County Kerry)

De Mórdha, Micheál, *Scéal agus Dán Oileáin, The Story and Fate of an Island* (Coiscéim, Dublin, 2012)

Flower, Robin, *The Western Island, The Great Blasket* (Oxford University Press, Oxford, 1944)

Fennelly, Anita, *Blasket Spirit, Stories from the Islands* (The Collins Press, Cork, 2009)

Gaunt, Carol O'Malley, *Hungry Hill: A Memoir* (University of Massachusetts Press, Amherst, Massachusetts, 2007)

Haughy, Anthony, *The Edge of Europe* (An Roinn Ealaíon Cultúir agus Gaeltachta, 1996)

Irish Independent, 'Islanders Plead for New Life on the Mainland', September 17, 1952

The Irish Press, 'Thugas Pionnt Dóibh' by Míceal Ó Ceárna, December, 1946

The Kerryman, 'Island Evacuation Impeded by Heavy Seas on Tuesday', November 21, 1953

The Kerryman, 'Evacuation Marks the End of an Era as Last Families Leave the Blaskets'*, November, 1953

Kanigel, Robert, *On an Irish Island* (Alfred A. Knopf, New York, 2012)

The National Archives of Ireland; *Islanders' Note to de Valera*, 18 September 1947

Ní Shúilleabháin, Brenda, *Bibeanna, Memories from a Corner of Ireland* (Mercier Press, Cork, 2007)

Ní Shúilleabháin, Eibhlis, *Letters from The Great Blasket* (Mercier Press, Cork, 2008)

Mac Conghail, Muiris, *The Blaskets: People and Literature – A Kerry Island Library* (Town House, Dublin, 1998)

Moreton, Cole, *Hungry for Home, Leaving the Blaskets: A Journey from the Edge of Ireland* (Viking Penguin, New York, 2000)

Matson, Leslie, *Tomás Ó Ceárnaigh: Biographical Notes* (Blasket Centre, 2008)

'Dingle – Ireland, Country Style', *National Geographic Traveler*, Summer 1986, Volume III, No. 2, pp. 60–67 (The National Geographic Society, New York, 1986)

Ó Criomhthain, Tomás, *Island Cross Talk, Pages from a Blasket Diary* (Oxford University Press, Oxford, 1986)

Ó Criomhthain, Tomás, *The Islandman* (Oxford University Press, Oxford, 1986)

Ó Guithín, Micheál, *A Pity Youth Does Not Last: Reminiscences of the Last Blasket Island Poet* (Oxford University Press, Oxford, 1982)

Ó Súilleabháin, Muiris, *Twenty Years a-Growing*, translated from Irish by Moya Llewelyn Davies and George Thomson (J.S. Sanders & Company, Nashville, Tennessee, 1998)

Office of the Houses of the Oireachtas, Historical Debates Website, http://historical-debates.oireachtas.ie

Reilly, Joan Morris, *Other Voices, Other Times . . . Hungry Hill Remembered* (Joan Morris Reilly, Springfield, Massachusetts, 2012)

Sayers, Peig, *Peig, The Autobiography of Peig Sayers of The Great Blasket Island*, Translated from Irish by Bryan MacMahon (Syracuse University Press, New York, 1974)

Sayers, Peig, *An Old Woman's Reflections, The Life of a Blasket Storyteller* (Oxford University Press, Oxford, 1962)

Stagles, Ray & Joan, *The Blasket Islands – Next Parish America* (O'Brien Press Ltd, Dublin, 1998)

Thomson, George, *Island Home, The Blasket Heritage* (Brandon Books, Dingle, County Kerry, 1998)

Tyers, Pádraig, *Blasket Memories, The Life of an Irish Island Community* (Mercier Press, Cork, 1998)

Tyers, Pádraig, *West Kerry Camera* (The Collins Press, Cork, 2006)

Ua Maoileoin, Pádraig, *The Blaskets* (Government Stationery Office, Dublin, 1994)

Index

Note: Page numbers in *italics* indicate photographs.

Index

From The Great Blasket to America